"I pledge to keep my body
and brain active this summer."

_____
Name

20___
Year

Let's Get Ready for First Grade!

Summer Fit Kindergarten to First Grade

Authors: Kelly Terrill and Portia Marin

Fitness and Nutrition: Lisa Roberts RN, BSN, PHN, James Cordova, Charles Miller, Steve Edwards, Missy Jones, Barbara Sherwood, John Bartlette, Malu Egido, Michael Ward

Healthy Family Lifestyle: Jay and Jen Jacobs & Marci and Courtney Crozier

Layout and Design: Scott Aucutt

Cover Design and Illustrations: Andy Carlson

Illustrations: Roxanne Ottley and Scott Aucutt

Series Created by George Starks

Summer Fit Dedication

Summer Fit is dedicated to Julia Hobbs and Carla Fisher who are the authors and unsung heroes of the original summer workbook series that helped establish the importance of summer learning. These women helped pioneer summer learning and dedicated their lives to teaching children and supporting parents. Carla and Julia made the world a better place by touching the lives of others using their love of education.

Summer Fit is also dedicated to Michael Starks whose presence is missed dearly, but who continues to teach us every day the importance of having courage in difficult times and treating others with respect, dignity, and a genuine concern for others.

Summer Fit Caution

If you have any questions regarding your child's ability to complete any of the suggested fitness activities consult your family doctor or child's pediatrician. Some of these exercises may require adult supervision. Children should stretch and warm up before exercises. Do not push children past their comfort level or ability. These physical fitness activities were created to be fun for parents and caregivers as well as the child, but not as a professional training or weight loss program. Exercise should stop immediately if you or your child experiences any of the following symptoms: pain, feeling dizzy or faint, nausea, or severe fatigue.

Summer Fit Copyright

Special thanks to the Terry Fox Foundation for use of Terry's photo and inspiring us all to contribute to making the world a better place for others each in our own way.

Printed in the USA
All Rights Reserved
ISBN: 978-0-9762800-7-1
www.SummerFitLearning.com

TABLE OF CONTENTS

Importance of Summer Learning and Fitness

Dear Parents,

Without opportunities to learn and practice essential skills over the summer months, most children fall behind academically. Research shows that summer learning loss varies, but that children can lose the equivalency of 2.5 months of math and 2 months of reading skills while away from school. In addition, children lose more than just academic knowledge during the summer. Research also shows that children are at greater risk of actually gaining more weight during summer vacation than during the school year:

FACT 1

All young people experience learning losses when they do not engage in educational activities during the summer. Research spanning 100 years shows that students typically score lower on standardized tests at the end of summer vacation than they do on the same tests at the beginning of the summer (White, 1906; Heyns, 1978; Entwisle & Alexander 1992; Cooper, 1996; Downey et al, 2004).

FACT 2

Research shows that children gain weight three times faster during the summer months – gaining as much weight during the summer as they do during the entire school year – even though the summertime is three times shorter. Von Hippel, P. T., Powell, B., Downey, D.B., & Rowland, N. (2007).

FACT 3

In the New York City school system, elementary and middle school students who placed in the top third of a fitness scale had better math and reading scores than students in the bottom third of the fitness scale. Those who were in the top 5% for fitness scored an average of 36 percentage points higher on state reading and math exams than did the least-fit 5%. New York City Department of Health. (2009)

Summer vacation is a great opportunity to use a variety of resources and programs to extend the academic learning experience and to reinforce life and social skills. It is an opportunity to give learning a different look and feel than what children are used to during the school year. Summer is a season that should be fun and carefree, but do not underestimate the opportunity and importance of helping children prepare for the upcoming school year. The key to a successful new school year is keeping your children active and learning this summer!

Sincerely,

Summer Fit Learning

FACT
You are your
child's greatest
teacher.

Inside Summer Fit

Purpose

The purpose of Summer Fit is to offer a comprehensive program for parents that promotes health and physical activity along side of academic and social skills. Summer Fit is designed to help create healthy and balanced family lifestyles.

Stay Smart

Summer Fit contains activities in reading, writing, math, language arts, and science.

Program Components

Summer Fit activities and exercises are divided into 10 sections to correlate with the traditional 10 weeks of summer. Each section begins with a weekly overview and incentive calendar so parents and children can talk about the week ahead while reviewing the previous week. There are 10 pages of activities for each week. The child does 2 pages a day that should take 20-30 minutes a day to complete. Each day offers a simple routine to reinforce basic skills and includes a physical fitness exercise and healthy habit. Each week also reinforces a core value on a daily basis to build character and social skills. Activities start off easy and progressively get more difficult so by the end of the workbook children are mentally, physically and socially prepared for the grade ahead.

Stay Cool

Summer Fit uses role models to reinforce the importance of good character and social skills.

Summer Fit includes a daily exercise program that children complete as part of their one-page of activities a day. These daily exercises and movement activities foster active lifestyles and get parents and children moving together.

Summer Fit uses daily value-based activities to reinforce good behavior.

Summer Fit promotes the body-brain connection and gives parents the tools to motivate children to use both.

Summer Fit includes an online component that gives children and parents additional summer learning and fitness resources at SummerFitLearning.com.

Summer Fit contains activities and exercises created by educators, parents and trainers committed to creating active learning environments that include movement and play as part of the learning experience.

Summer Fit uses role models from around the world to introduce and reinforce core values and the importance of good behavior.

Stay Active

Summer Fit uses a daily fitness exercise and wellness tips to keep children moving and having fun.

Teaching the Whole Child

The Whole Child philosophy is based on the belief that every child should be healthy, engaged, supported and challenged in all aspects of their lives. Investing in the *overall* development of your child is critical to their personal health and well being. There is increased awareness that a balanced approach to nurturing and teaching our children will benefit all aspects of their lives; therefore creating well rounded students who are better equipped to successfully navigate the ups and downs of their education careers.

Supports Common Core Standards

The Common Core provides teachers and parents with a common understanding of what students are expected to learn. These standards will provide appropriate benchmarks for all students, regardless of where they live and be applied for students in grades K-12. Summer Fit is aligned to Common Core Standards.

Learn more at: CoreStandards.org

Top 5 Parent Summer Tips

1 Routine: Set a time and a place for your child to complete their activities and exercises each day.

2 Balance: Use a combination of resources to reinforce basic skills in fun ways. Integrate technology with traditional learning, but do not replace one with another.

3 Motivate and Encourage: Inspire your child to complete their daily activities and exercises. Get excited and show your support of their accomplishments!

4 Play as a Family: Slap "high 5," jump up and down and get silly! Show how fun it is to be active by doing it yourself! Health Experts recommend 60 minutes of play a day and kids love seeing parents playing and having fun!

5 Eat Healthy (and together): Kids are more likely to eat less healthy during the summer, than during the school year. Put food back on the table and eat together at least once a day.

Health and Wellness in the Home

Physical activity is critical to your child's health and well-being. Research shows that children with better health are in school more days, learn better, have higher self esteem and lower risk of developing chronic diseases.

Exercise Provides:

✔ Stronger muscles and bones

✔ Leaner body because exercise helps control body fat

✔ Increased blood flow to the brain and wellness at home

✔ Lower blood pressure and blood cholesterol levels

✔ Kids who are active are less likely to develop weight issues, display more self-confidence, perform better academically and enjoy a better overall quality of life!

Tips from a former *Biggest Loser*

Marci Crozier
Former contestant of NBC's
The Biggest Loser

Marci Crozier lost 86 pounds on Season 11 of NBC's *The Biggest Loser*.

Sedentary lifestyles, weight issues and unhealthy habits need to be addressed at home. It is more likely that your child will include healthy habits as part of their everyday life if they understand:

✔ Why staying active and eating healthy is important

✔ What are healthy habits and what are not

✔ How to be healthy, active and happy

Go to the Health and Wellness Index in the back of the book for more Family Health and Wellness Tips.

Warm Up!

It is always best to prepare your body for any physical activity by moving around and stretching.

Get Loose! Stretch!

Move your head from side to side, trying to touch each shoulder. Now move your head forward, touching your chin to your chest and then looking up and back as far as you can, trying to touch your back with the back of your head.

Touch your toes when standing, bend over at the waist and touch the end of your toes or the floor. Hold this for 10 seconds.

Get Moving

Walk or jog for 3-5 minutes to warm up before you exercise. Shake your arms and roll your shoulders when you are finished walking or jogging.

A healthy diet and daily exercise will maximize the likelihood of children growing up healthy and strong. Children are still growing and adding bone mass, so a balanced diet is very important to their overall health. Provide three nutritious meals a day that include fruits and vegetables. Try to limit fast food consumption, and find time to cook more at home where you know the source of your food and how your food is prepared. Provide your child with healthy, well-portioned snacks, and try to keep them from eating too much at a time.

SCORE! A HEALTHY EATING GOAL

As a rule of thumb, avoid foods and drinks that are high in sugars, fat, or caffeine. Try to provide fruits, vegetables, grains, lean meats, chicken, fish, and low-fat dairy products as part of a healthy meal when possible. Obesity and being overweight, even in children, can significantly increase the risk of heart disease, diabetes, and other chronic illnesses. Creating an active lifestyle this summer that includes healthy eating and exercise will help your child maintain a healthy weight and protect them from certain illnesses throughout the year.

Let's Eat Healthy!

5 Steps to Improve Eating Habits of Your Family

1) Make fresh fruits and veggies readily available.

2) Cook more at home, and sit down for dinner as a family.

3) Limit consumption of soda, desserts and sugary cereals.

4) Serve smaller portions.

5) Limit snacks to just one or two daily.

Technology and Child Development

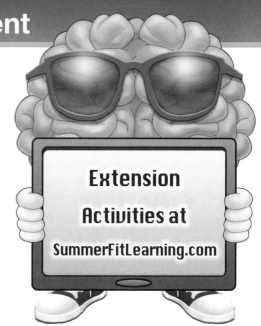

Children start developing initiative and creativity at a young age. Technology offers children additional outlets to learn and demonstrate their creativity. However, it is critical that active playtime and traditional learning resources including crayons, paint, books and toys are included as an essential part of the child's daily routine in addition to technology use. Used appropriately, computers can be a positive element of children's play and learning as they explore and experiment. Screen time (including TV, computer, phone and games) should be limited to a maximum of one to two hours per day for young children (American Academy of Pediatrics).

Extension Activities at SummerFitLearning.com

3 KEYS TO TECH SUCCESS

1 Consider technology as one tool among many used to enhance learning, not as a replacement for child interactions with each other, with adults, or other modes of learning.

2 Explore touch screens with a wide variety of appropriate interactive media experiences with your child. Verbally communicate with them the concepts of the game or apps that engage them. Express interest and encouragement of their performance.

3 Establish "No Screen Zones" for children such as the dinner table at home and in public settings. Screens create barriers that are difficult to talk through and can easily isolate children and parents. Establishing appropriate times and places to use technology will help children develop "tech-etiquette."

Core Values in the Home

Understanding core values allows your child to have a clearer understanding of their own behavior in your home, in their classroom and in our communities. Core values are fundamental to society and are incorporated into our civil laws, but are taught first and foremost at home. Parents and guardians are the most important and influential people in a child's life. It is up to you to raise children who respect and accept themselves, and others around them.

Role Models

A role model is a person who serves as an example of a particular value or trait. There are many people today, and throughout history, who exemplify in their own actions the values that we strive to have ourselves, and teach our children.

Mahatma Ghandi
Advocate for non-violence

RESPECT

UNDERGROUND R.R.

TRUSTWORTHY

Harriet Tubman
Civil Rights Activist

Bullying

In recent years, bullying has become a leading topic of concern. It is a complex issue, and can be difficult for parents to know what to do when they hear that their child is being bullied or is bullying others. Bullying is always wrong. It is critical that you intervene appropriately when bullying occurs. Make sure your child understands what bullying means. Check in with your child often to make sure he/she knows you are interested and aware of what is going on in their social lives.

Learn more at StopBullying.gov

HONESTY

Abraham Lincoln
16th President of the United States

Books Build Better Brains!

Reading is considered the gateway to all learning, so it is critical as a parent or caregiver to assist and encourage children to read at all grade levels regardless of reading ability.

1. Create a daily reading routine. A reading routine provides the practice a child needs to reinforce and build reading and literacy skills.

2. Create a summer reading list. Choose a variety of children's books, including fairy tales, poems, fiction and non-fiction books.

3. Join or start a summer reading club. Check your local public library or bookstore.

4. Talk with your child about a book that you are reading. Let your child see how much you enjoy reading and ask them to share stories from some of their favorite books.

5. Children love to hear stories about their family. Tell your child what it was like when you or your parents were growing up, or talk about a funny thing that happened when you were their age. Have them share stories of their own about when they were "young."

Read 20 minutes a day!

CYBER READERS: Books in a Digital World

With the amount of electronic resources available, children are gaining access to subjects faster than ever before. With electronic resources comes a significant amount of "screen time" that children spend with technology including television, movies, computers, phones and gaming systems. It is important to manage "screen time" and include time for books. Reading a book helps develop attention spans and allows children to build their imaginations without the aid of animated graphics, special effects and sound that may hinder a child's ability to create these for themselves.

Summer Reading List – Kindergarten to First Grade

The key to a good summer reading list is having a wide variety of books. Visit the library and let your child choose titles of their own and ask the librarian for recommendations.

Color the  for every title read and the **Book Report activity page** (in the back of the book) is completed. Go to SummerFitLearning.com to download and print out more **Book Report activity pages** to complete.

Fairy tales, folk tales, and nursery rhymes including: "Cinderella," "The Gingerbread Man," "Little Red Riding Hood," "The Three Little Pigs," "The Three Billy Goats Gruff," "Goldilocks and the Three Bears," and "Mother Goose Rhymes"

The Berenstain Bears
Berenstain, Stan and Jan

Curious George
Rey, H.A.

Clifford, the Big Red Dog
Bridwell, Norman

Miss Nelson Is Missing!
Allard, Harry

Goodnight, Moon
Brown, Margaret W.

Draw Draw Draw
Ames, Lee J

Make Way for Ducklings
McCloskey, Robert

The Tale of Peter Rabbit
Potter, Beatrix

Harry the Dirty Dog
Zion, Gene

There's a Nightmare in My Closet
Mayer, Mercer

Madeline
Bemelmans, Ludwig

Where the Wild Things Are
Sendak, Maurice

Caps for Sale
Solbodkina, Esphyr

The Very Hungry Caterpillar
Carle, Eric

The Cat in the Hat
Seuss, Dr.

The Little Engine That Could
Piper, Watty

Ira Sleeps Over
Waber, Bernard

Parents: some of the test is oral. A place has been given to record your child's answer.

Oral Count to 20. My child can count to _____.

Say these numbers. (Circle any your child cannot recall).

9	1	8	6	7	3	2	5	4	10

Write the numbers 1 to 10.

_____

- -

_____

Name these shapes.

○	△	☐	▭

- Color the circle red
- Color the triangle blue

- Color the square green
- Color the rectangle orange

Draw a circle		Draw a square	
Draw a triangle		Draw a rectangle	

Draw a line to connect the dots.

•   •

☺ ☺ ☺ ☺ ☺	How many smiley faces? _____
♥ ♥	How many hearts? _____
★ ★ ★ ★	How many stars? _____

What shape has the most? _____

What shape has the least? _____

What time is it? (oral)

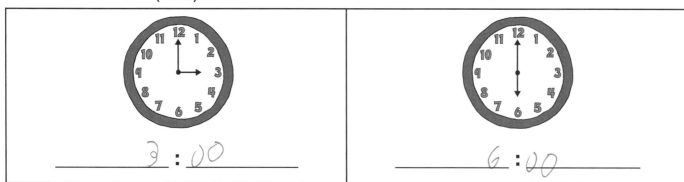

_____ 3 : 00   _____ 6 : 00

Name these coins.

_____   _____   _____

Can you tell me the value of each coin?

_____   _____   _____

Name and continue the pattern.

      _____

Look at the shapes.

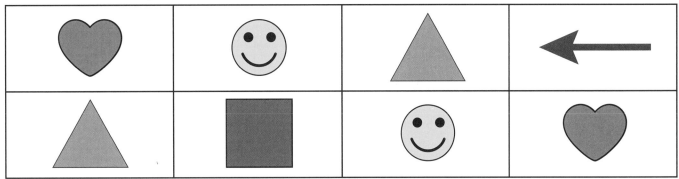

Circle the shape that is below the heart.

Draw a blue X on the shape that is above the square.

Underline the shape that is between a smiley face and an arrow.

Circle the group that has more.

Say the days of the week in order.

Sunday _____ Monday _____ Tuesday _____ Wednesday _____

Thursday _____ Friday _____ Saturday _____.

Ask your child to circle the picture that doesn't belong in each row.

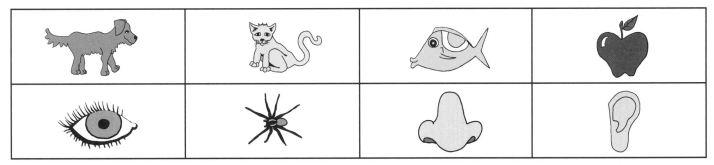

Skills Assessment Kindergarten

Name the uppercase and lowercase letters.

A a	B b	C c	D d	E e	F f	G g	H h	I i	J j	K k	L l	M m
N n	O o	P p	Q q	R r	S s	T t	U u	V v	W w	X x	Y y	Z z

Ask about a mix of uppercase and lowercase to be sure they are recognizing both. Circle any letters your child does not know.

Point to each letter and ask your child to give the consonant or short vowel sound for each.

Tell me the sound you hear at the beginning of each word.

table _____   lamp _____   boy _____   rat _____

door _____   fly _____   cup _____   lock _____

Tell me the sound you hear at the end of each word.

box _____   ball _____   ham _____   dog _____

bus _____   sun _____   cat _____   star _____

I will say the sounds that make up each word and you tell me the word. For example, /c/ /u/ /p/ is the word cup. Say each individual sound and have your child blend them together.

/m/ /a/ /n/ = _____   /b/ /u/ /g/ = _____

/g/ /a/ /t/ /e/ = _____   /s/ /t/ /a/ /r/ = _____

WEEK 1

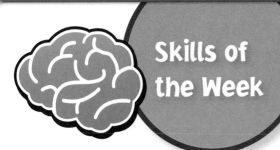

Skills of the Week

- ✔ Colors
- ✔ Numbers 1-20
- ✔ Beginning sounds
- ✔ Missing numbers
- ✔ Count the set
- ✔ Comparison of size
- ✔ Animal homes
- ✔ Circles

Honesty

Abraham Lincoln

Honesty means being fair, truthful, and trustworthy. Honesty means telling the truth no matter what. People who are honest do not lie, cheat, or steal.

Sometimes it is not easy to tell the truth, especially when you are scared and do not want to get in trouble or let others down. Try to remember that even when it is difficult telling the truth is always the best way to handle any situation and people will respect you more.

GET FIT TIME!

Play Every Day!

Weekly Extension Activities at SummerFitLearning.com

Honesty In Action!
Color the star each day you show honesty through your own actions.

17

WEEK 1 HEALTHY MIND + HEALTHY BODY

Color the ⭐ As You Complete Your Daily Task

	Day 1	Day 2	Day 3	Day 4	Day 5
MIND	☆	☆	☆	☆	☆
BODY	☆	☆	☆	☆	☆
DAILY READING	☆ 20 minutes	☆ 20 minutes	☆ 20 minutes	☆ 20 minutes	☆ 20 minutes

"I am honest"

"You Can do It"

_____
Print Name

Trace the words, color the correct color.

Red

Yellow

Black

Orange

Green

Blue

Brown

WEEK 1

DAY 1

Aerobic
Go to www.summerfitlearning.com for more Activities!

Exercise for today
Tag
Color the star when you complete each level.

☆ 10-30 Seconds
☆ 31-60 Seconds
☆ 61-90 Seconds

Be Healthy!
Eat an apple!

 Learn Your Numbers -

1. Trace the numbers, finish the rows.

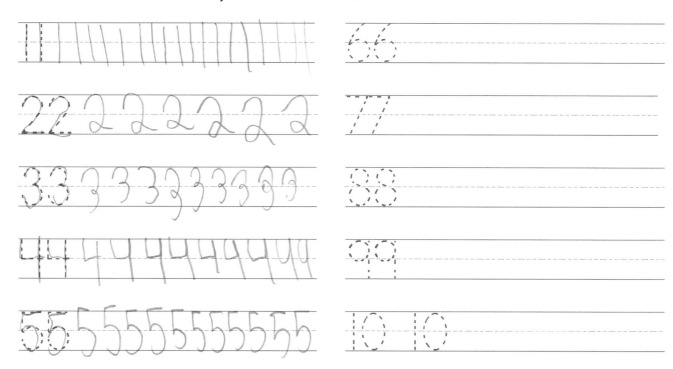

1 1 | 6 6
2 2 | 7 7
3 3 | 8 8
4 4 | 9 9
5 5 | 10 10

1+2=3 **Numbers and Math**

2. Starting from the left

Circle the 4th peanut.

  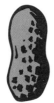 

3. How many cents? _____ ¢

Beginning Sounds Honesty

Circle the pictures that begin with the letter shown.

D

C

B

G

F

H

WEEK 1

DAY 2

Exercise for today
Leg Scissors
Color the star when you complete each level.

☆ 1-5 Reps
☆ 6-10 Reps
☆ 10-20 Reps

Be Healthy!
Fresh fruits come from your garden or a farm.

Count and Write - Fill in the missing numbers

1. Fill in the missing numbers.

1 , ___ , ___ , ___ , 5 , ___ , ___ , ___ , 0 ,

2. Count each set. Write how many.

_____

_____

_____

Draw a line from each picture to the letter that makes its beginning sound.

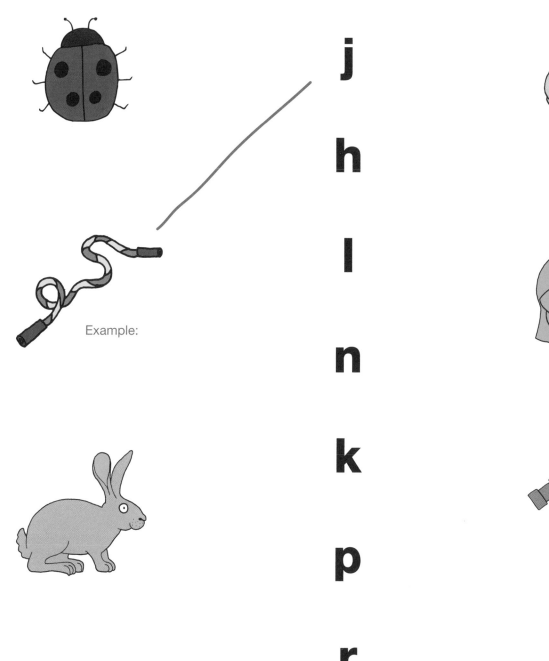

j

h

l

n

k

p

r

m

Example:

Aerobic Go to www.summerfitlearning.com for more Activities!

Exercise for today
Foot Bag
Color the star when you complete each level.

☆ 10-30 Seconds
☆ 31-60 Seconds
☆ 61-90 Seconds

Be Healthy!
Walnuts look like a brain- they make you smart!

Count and Write - Fill in the missing numbers

Trace the numbers, finish the rows.

1. Circle the taller tree.	2. Circle the smaller mouse.

3. Circle the longest worm.

© Summer Fit

Where do I live? Draw a line from each animal to the home it lives in.

Example:

WEEK 1

DAY 4

Strength
Go to www.summerfitlearning.com for more Activities!

Exercise for today
Ankle Touches
Color the star when you complete each level.

 1-5 Reps
6-10 Reps
10-20 Reps

Be Healthy!
Breakfast is very important!

 Geometry and Shapes

 **1. Trace the name of this shape.**   Circle

2. How many sides? _____ **How many vertexes (corners)?** _____

4. Trace and draw the circle.

_____   _____

5. Finish the pattern.

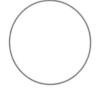

_____

6. How many circles do you see?

_____

© Summer Fit

Honesty means to tell the truth.

Abraham Lincoln

Abraham Lincoln was known as "Honest Abe" because he always told the truth. He was a tall man who wore a tall hat, but people remember him for his honesty. He was a great leader because he was honest and trustworthy.

Draw how it feels to tell the truth. Draw how it feels to lie.

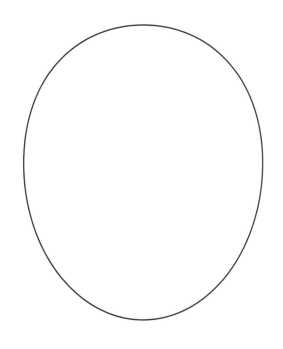

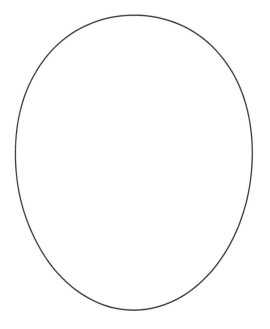

"Believe in yourself!"

Choose 1 or more activities to do with your family or friends. Color today's star when you are finished. Good job!

☐ Make masks of different animals or people using paper plates and popsicle sticks. Pretend to be someone different, then take off the mask and be yourself.

☐ Play a game like checkers with a friend or family member. Make sure to play fair.

☐ Draw a picture of Abraham Lincoln. On his tall hat have your parents write "Honesty is the best policy." Talk about what that means.

Core Value Book List
Read More About Honesty

The Tale of Peter Rabbit
By Beatrix Potter

Pinocchio
By C. Collodi

Dandelion
By Don Freeman

Reading Extension Activities at SummerFitLearning.com

Let's Talk About It

Children sometimes have a hard time distinguishing between what is real and what is made up. Practice telling things the way they really are and pointing out things that are made up or partially real. Encourage complete honesty and avoid confrontation when trying to get to the truth. Be mindful of little white lies. It is hard for kids to understand "good lies" vs. "bad lies." For example, when giving your child medicine, instead of saying, "It doesn't taste that bad," you could say, "This will help you feel better."

Play Time!
Choose a Game or Activity to Play for 60 minutes today!

YOU CHOOSE

_____
Write down which game or activity you played today!

Watch exercise videos at www.summerfitlearning.com

Be Healthy!
Name a fruit or vegetable that is green.

© Summer Fit

WEEK 2

PARENT GUIDE WEEK 2

Skills of the Week

✔ Beginning sounds
✔ Counting sets
✔ Before and after
✔ Missing numbers
✔ Time
✔ Short a
✔ Short e
✔ Count back from 10
✔ Rhyming words
✔ Squares

Compassion

Mother Teresa

Compassion is caring about the feelings and needs of others.

Sometimes we are so focussed on our own feelings that we don't care how other people feel. If we consider other's feelings before our own, the world can be a much kinder place. Take time to do something nice for another person and you will feel better about yourself.

Play Every Day!

Weekly Extension Activities at SummerFitLearning.com

Compassion In Action!
Color the star each day you show compassion through your own actions.

WEEK 2

Color the ⭐ As You Complete Your Daily Task

	Day 1	Day 2	Day 3	Day 4	Day 5
MIND	⭐	⭐	⭐	⭐	⭐
BODY	⭐	⭐	⭐	⭐	⭐
DAILY READING	⭐ 20 minutes	⭐ 20 minutes	⭐ 20 minutes	⭐ 20 minutes	⭐ 20 minutes

"I am compassionate"

"You Can do It"

_____
Print Name

Circle the letter that begins each picture.

t d r	p b r	g w j

v y z	b l m	n p t
q s p	n m l	z j g
z t v	s w m	d t r

WEEK 2

DAY 1

Exercise for today
Tree Sprints
Color the star when you complete each level.

☆ **10-30 Seconds**
☆ 31-60 Seconds
☆ **61-90 Seconds**

Be Healthy!
Each color vegetable gives you a different power to be healthy!

WEEK 2

DAY 1

1+2=3
⊕ ⊖
⊗ ⊘ =

Counting, Before and After

1. | Color 6 | Color 9

2. What number comes before?

| _____, 2 | _____, 6 | _____, 10 |

3. What number comes after?

| 8, _____ | 11, _____ | 19, _____ |

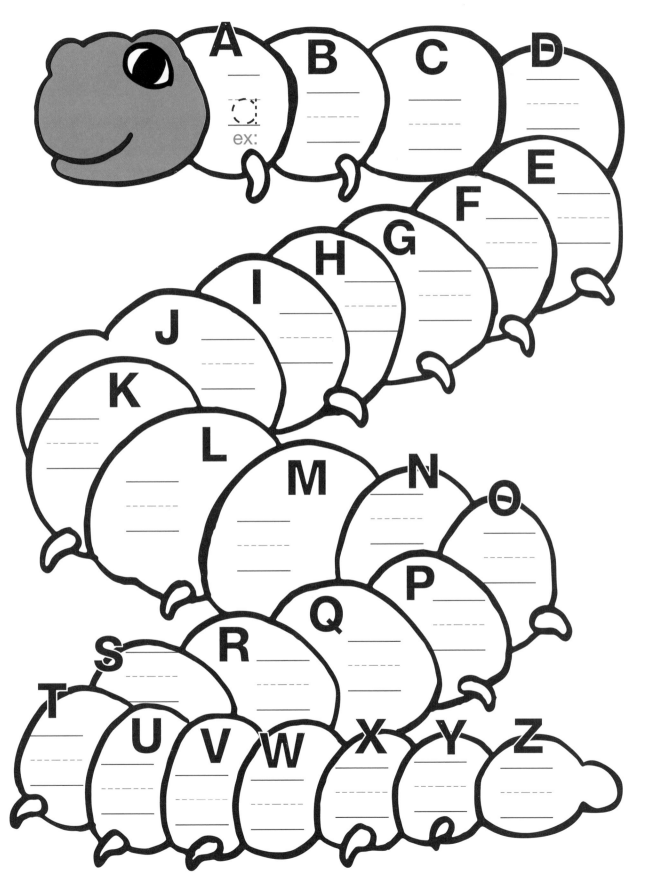

A
ex:

B

C

D

E

F

G

H

I

J

K

L

M

N

O

P

Q

R

S

T

U

V

W

X

Y

Z

Exercise for today
Push-ups

Color the star when you complete each level.

☆ **1-5 Reps**
☆ **6-10 Reps**
☆ **10-20 Reps**

WEEK 2

DAY 2

 Time and Numbers - Missing numbers.

1. Write the missing numbers on the clock.

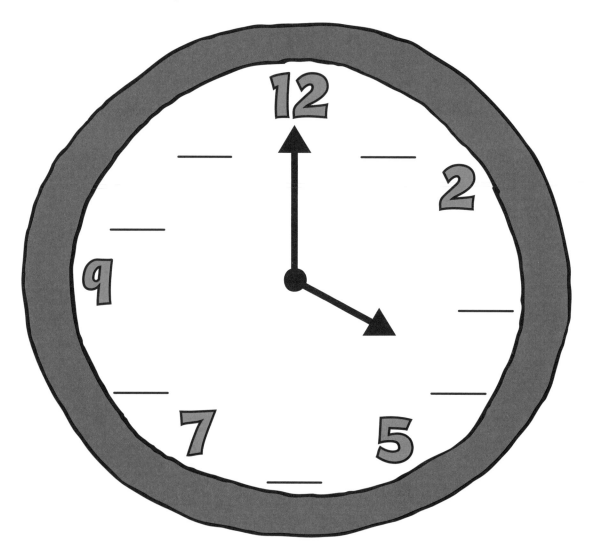

2. What time is it? _____ o'clock.

© Summer Fit

Letters and Sounds - "Short a and e"   **Compassion**

Circle the pictures in each row that have the same vowel sound as the first picture.

WEEK 2

DAY 3

Aerobic

Go to www.summerfitlearning.com for more Activities!

Exercise for today
Jumping Jacks
Color the star when you complete each level.

☆ **10-30 Seconds**
☆ 31-60 Seconds
☆ 61-90 Seconds

Be Healthy!
Make popsicles out of your favorite fruit juice!

 Count and Write

Count the spots on each ladybug.
Draw a line to match the number.

1.

2

8

4.

2.

6

10

5.

3.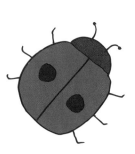

4

12

6.

7. **Count backwards. Fill in the missing numbers.**

10, _____, 8, _____, 6, _____, 4, _____, 2, _____, 0

WEEK 2

DAY 3

36 © Summer Fit

Draw a line to match the pictures that rhyme.

1. 　　　　　　　　　　　

2. 　　　　　　　　　　　

3. 　　　　　　　　　　　

4. 　　　　　　　　　　　

5. 　　　　　　　　　　　

Exercise for today
Moon Touches
Color the star when you complete each level.

☆ **1-5 Reps**
☆ **6-10 Reps**
☆ **10-20 Reps**

Be Healthy!
Cook a meal with your family today.

WEEK 2

DAY 4

 Geometry

1. Trace the name of this shape.

2. How many sides? _____ **How many vertexes (corners)?** _____

4. Trace and draw the square.

_____   _____

5. Finish the pattern.

_____

5. Circle the smallest circle.

© Summer Fit

Compassion is caring about others.

Mother Teresa

Mother Teresa helped many sick and poor people in India. She took care of people who had nobody else to care for them. Mother Teresa spent her life helping people. She cared for everyone she met. She treated others the way she wanted to be treated.

I show compassion by caring for people, animals and the earth.

Helping people makes me happy. Draw a picture of yourself helping a friend who fell off the swing and is crying.

"Believe in yourself!"

Choose 1 or more activities to do with your family or friends. Color today's star when you are finished. Good job!

☐ Make a card for someone who is sick.

☐ Care about the earth. Go on a "garbage walk" around your neighborhood. Pick up all the garbage you find in your neighborhood or park.

☐ Say something nice to someone who has been mean to you, or think of someone you have been unkind to. Say you are sorry and ask them to forgive you.

Core Value Book List
Read More About Compassion

Biscuit Finds a Friend
By Alyssa Satin Capucilli

Owen
By Kevin Henkes

Ibis, a True Wale Story
By John Himmelman

Reading Extension Activities at SummerFitLearning.com

Let's Talk About It

Learning about compassion early in life builds moral character and fosters self-confidence. Teach your child compassion by modeling compassion. Give them opportunities to be responsible and help around the house. Help them become aware of the feelings of others by talking and role playing. Ask questions like "How would you feel if..?" Ask them to put themselves in someone else's shoes. For example, "How would you feel if your best friend moved away?"

Play Time!
Choose a Game or Activity to Play for 60 minutes today!

YOU CHOOSE

_____

Write down which game or activity you played today!

Watch exercise videos at www.summerfitlearning.com

Be Healthy!
Wash your hands.

WEEK 3

Skills of the Week

- ✔ Capital letters
- ✔ More than, less than
- ✔ Measurement
- ✔ Time
- ✔ Ending sounds
- ✔ Cross off to take away
- ✔ Days of the week
- ✔ Triangles
- ✔ Patterns

Trustworthiness

Harriet Tubman

Trustworthiness is being worthy of trust. It means people can count on you.

You are honest and you keep your word. Sometimes it is easy to forget what we tell people because we try to do too much or we are constantly moving around. Try to slow down and follow through on what you say before moving onto something else.

GET FIT TIME!

Play Every Day!

Weekly Extension Activities at SummerFitLearning.com

Trust In Action!
Color the star each day you show trustworthiness through your own actions.

41

WEEK 3

Color the ⭐ As You Complete Your Daily Task

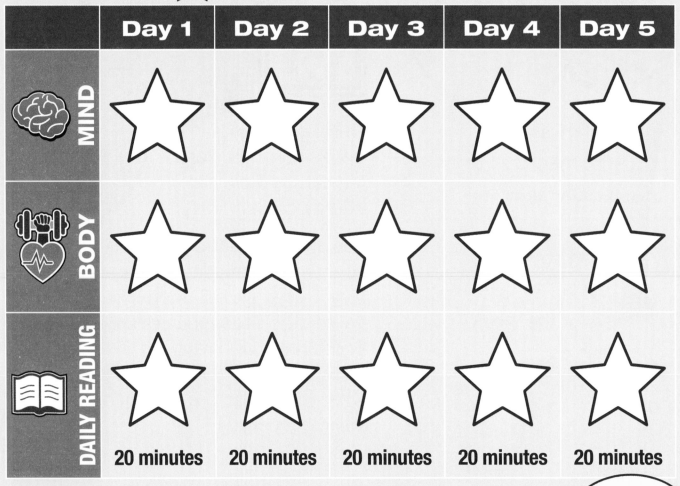

	Day 1	Day 2	Day 3	Day 4	Day 5
MIND	☆	☆	☆	☆	☆
BODY	☆	☆	☆	☆	☆
DAILY READING	☆	☆	☆	☆	☆
	20 minutes	20 minutes	20 minutes	20 minutes	20 minutes

"You Can do It"

"I am trustworthy"

_____
Print Name

Write the capital letter next to each lower case letter.

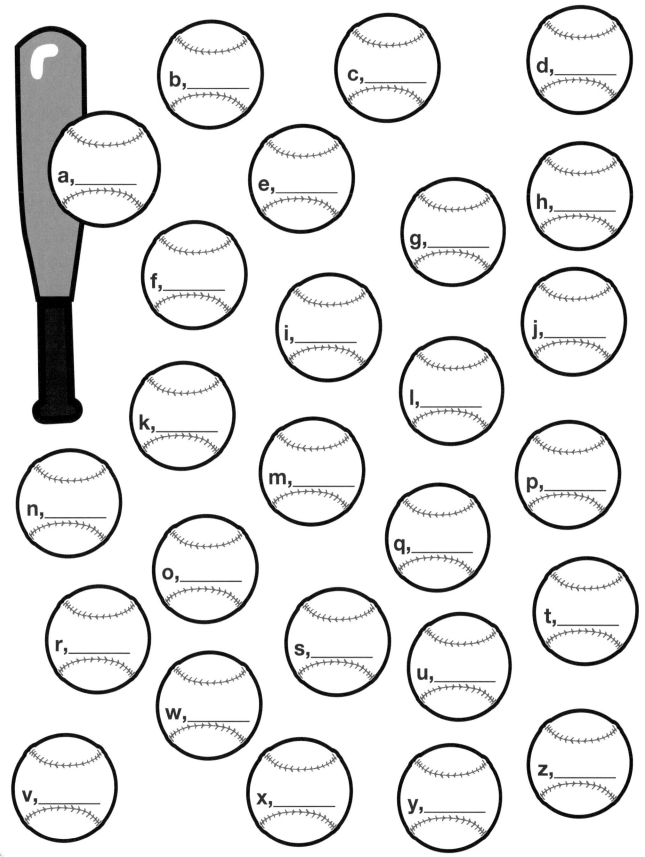

a,_____
b,_____
c,_____
d,_____
e,_____
f,_____
g,_____
h,_____
i,_____
j,_____
k,_____
l,_____
m,_____
n,_____
o,_____
p,_____
q,_____
r,_____
s,_____
t,_____
u,_____
v,_____
w,_____
x,_____
y,_____
z,_____

 **Aerobic**  Go to www.summerfitlearning.com for more Activities!

Exercise for today
Cross-Country Skier
Color the star when you complete each level.

☆ **10-30 Seconds**
☆ 31-60 Seconds
☆ **61-90 Seconds**

 **Be Healthy!** Instead of juice, mix a piece of fruit with water.

WEEK 3

 More than, less than

1. Circle the set that has more.

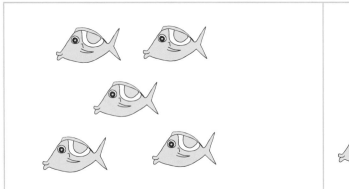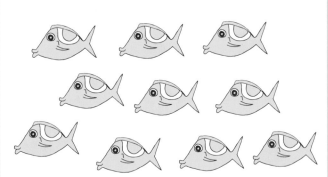

2. How many fish all together?

$$5 + 10 = \underline{\hspace{3cm}}$$

3. Cross off the set that has less.

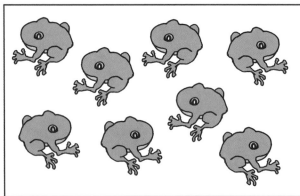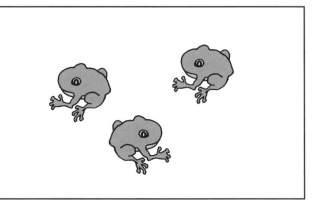

4. How many frogs all together?

$$8 + 3 = \underline{\hspace{3cm}}$$

DAY 1

Living things need air, water, and food. People, animals and plants are living things. Circle the pictures of living things.

Strength
Go to www.summerfitlearning.com for more Activities!

Exercise for today
Chop and Squat
Color the star when you complete each level.

☆ **1-5 Reps**
☆ **6-10 Reps**
☆ **10-20 Reps**

Be Healthy!
Instead of a sweet, try toast with cream cheese or peanut butter!

 Measurement

1. Start at the right. Circle the eighth peach.

2. Look at each clock, write the time shown.

_____:_____   _____:_____

3. Measure the length of the line.

The line is _____ paperclips long.

4. Circle the shorter flower.

5. Which weighs more?

46   © Summer Fit

Say the name of each picture. Listen for the ending sound.
Circle the letter that makes the ending sound.

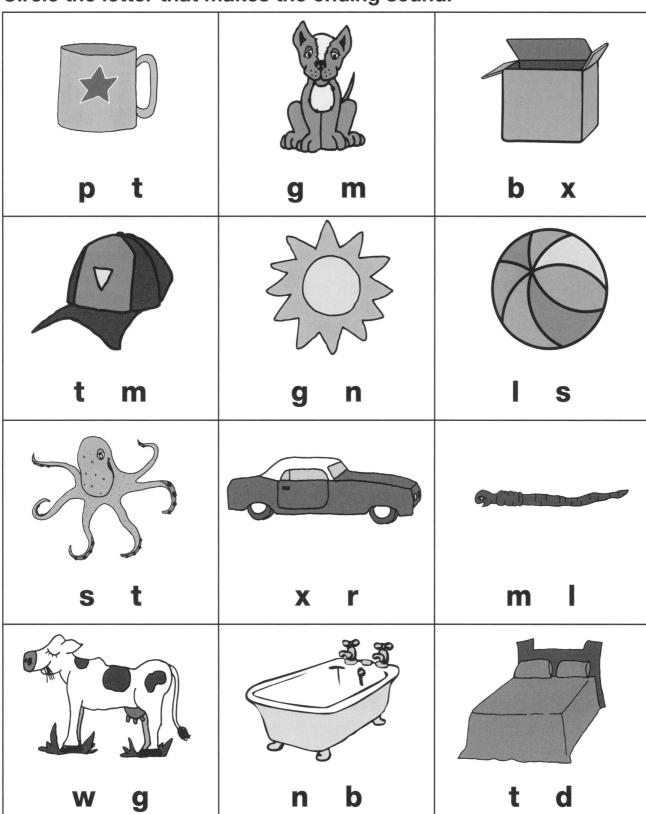

p t	g m	b x
t m	g n	l s
s t	x r	m l
w g	n b	t d

WEEK 3

DAY 3

Aerobic

Go to www.summerfitlearning.com for more Activities!

Exercise for today
Hide and Seek
Color the star when you complete each level.

☆ 10-30 Seconds
☆ 31-60 Seconds
☆ 61-90 Seconds

WEEK 3

Math - Cross off to take away

1.

Cross 3 out. How many are left? 6 - 3 = _____

2.

Cross 5 out. How many are left? 10 - 5 = _____

3.

Cross 1 out. 5 - 1 = _____

4.

Cross 6 out. 12 - 6 = _____

DAY 3

© Summer Fit

Sunday
Monday
Tuesday
Wednesday
Thursday
Friday
Saturday

Write the name of your favorite day of the week.

_____

- -

_____

Draw something you like to do on that day.

Strength

 Go to www.summerfitlearning.com for more Activities!

Exercise for today
Fly in the Ointment
Color the star when you complete each level.

☆ 1-5 Reps
☆ 6-10 Reps
☆ 10-20 Reps

Be Healthy!
Take a walk with your parents today.

WEEK 3

DAY 4

 **Geometry**

1. Trace the name of this shape. Triangle

2. How many sides? _____ **How many vertexes (corners)?** _____

4. Trace and draw the triangle.

 _____ _____

5. Finish the pattern.

50 © Summer Fit

Being Trustworthy means keeping your promises.

Harriet Tubman

Harriet Tubman escaped from slavery and helped many other slaves escape too. Harriet helped others using the "Underground Railroad" which was a secret escape route for slaves. Many people hated slavery and supported Harriet as she led people to freedom. People trusted Harriet with their lives and she did not let them down.

Color the word TRUSTWORTHY

TRUSTWORTHY

"Believe in yourself!"

Choose 1 or more activities to do with your family or friends. Color today's star when you are finished. Good job!

☐ When I am trustworthy I am being a good friend. Make a card for a friend.

☐ Make up a song about being trustworthy. Share it with your family and friends.

☐ Being trustworthy means you keep your word and don't break promises. Make a sign or poster that says, "You can count on me." This week practice keeping all your promises.

Core Value Book List
Read More About Trust

Apples and the Arrow
By Mary and Conrad Buff

A Day's Work
By Eve Bunting

Andy and the Lion
By James Daugherty

Reading Extension Activities at SummerFitLearning.com

Let's Talk About It

Only make promises you plan to keep. Tell the truth to and in front of your child, and remember to be consistent. When watching movies or tv shows with your child, discuss ways the characters are trustworthy and the ways they are not.

Stepping Stones

Stepping Stones Entertainment™ was founded by parents who wanted to provide meaningful family movies to help inspire common values. It is made up of people from many different backgrounds, nationalities and beliefs. For more than 20 years, Stepping Stones has provided families with movies about integrity, charity, forgiveness and many other common values through hundreds of films for all ages. Learn more at **www.steppingstones.com**.

STEPPING STONES.COM
Meaningful Family Movies

Play Time!
Choose a Game or Activity to Play for 60 minutes today!

YOU CHOOSE

_____
Write down which game or activity you played today!

Watch exercise videos at www.summerfitlearning.com

Be Healthy!
Plant a family garden and eat what you grow.

Skills of the Week

Self-Discipline

- ✔ Short u
- ✔ Charts and graphs
- ✔ Counting sets
- ✔ Classifying
- ✔ Tens and ones
- ✔ Short i
- ✔ Dot-to-dot 1-20
- ✔ 5 Senses
- ✔ Rectangles
- ✔ Patterns

Stephanie Lopez Cox

Self-discipline means self-control. It is working hard and getting yourself to do what is important.

It is easy to lose interest in what you are doing, especially if it does not come fast and easy. Focus your attention on what you are trying to accomplish and try to block out other things until you reach your goal.

Play Every Day!

Weekly Extension Activities at SummerFitLearning.com

Self-Discipline In Action!
Color the star each day you show self-discipline through your own actions.

WEEK 4
HEALTHY MIND + HEALTHY BODY

Color the ⭐ As You Complete Your Daily Task

	Day 1	Day 2	Day 3	Day 4	Day 5
MIND	⭐	⭐	⭐	⭐	⭐
BODY	⭐	⭐	⭐	⭐	⭐
DAILY READING	⭐ 20 minutes	⭐ 20 minutes	⭐ 20 minutes	⭐ 20 minutes	⭐ 20 minutes

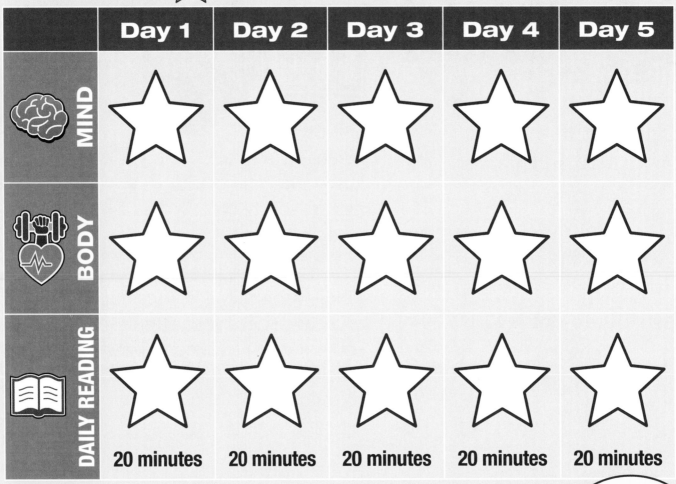

"You Can do It"

"I am self-disciplined"

_____
Print Name

Color the pictures that have the short u sound as in "umbrella"

Exercise for today
Turtle and Rabbit
Color the star when you complete each level.

☆ 10-30 Seconds
☆ 31-60 Seconds
☆ 61-90 Seconds

Be Healthy!
Try a new food today.

WEEK 4

DAY 1

Charts and graphs

Count the pictures to complete the bar graph.

Camel example:	▓	▓					
Rhino							
Giraffe							
Porcupine							
Elephant							
	0	1	2	3	4	5	6

How many 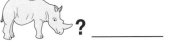? _____

How many ? _____

How many ? _____

How many ? _____

How many ? _____

Cross out the picture in each row that doesn't belong.

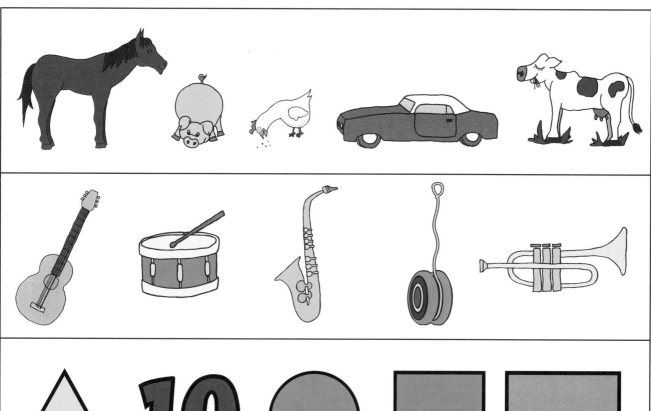

WEEK 4

DAY 2

Strength
Go to www.summerfitlearning.com for more Activities!

Exercise for today
Jumping Jacks
Color the star when you complete each level.

☆ **1-5 Reps**
☆ **6-10 Reps**
☆ **10-20 Reps**

Be Healthy!
Brush your teeth twice a day.

1+2=3

Numbers and Math - Tens and ones

Write how many tens and ones for each picture.

1.

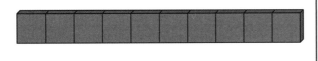

_____ tens

_____ ones

2.

_____ tens

_____ ones

3.

_____ tens

_____ ones

4.

_____ tens

_____ ones

© Summer Fit

Circle the pictures that have a short i sound as in bib.

Exercise for today
Wheel Over
Color the star when you complete each level.

☆ **10-30 Seconds**
☆ 31-60 Seconds
☆ **61-90 Seconds**

Be Healthy!
Eat your snack at the table, not in front of the computer or television.

Connect the Dots - Count from 1 to 20. Color the picture.

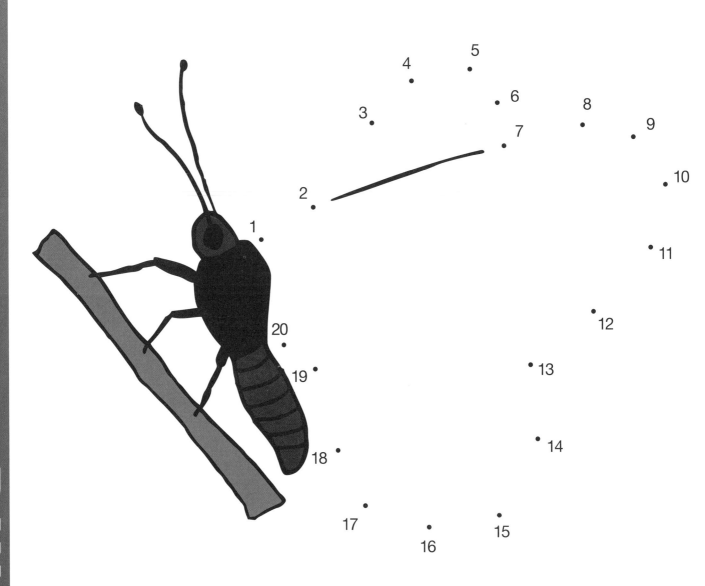

Trace the words, draw a line to the correct picture.

I 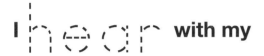 **with my**

I  **with my**

I 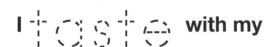 **with my**

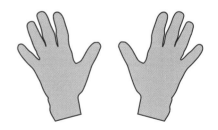

I taste **with my**

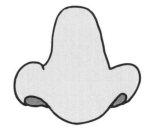

I touch **with my**

WEEK 4

DAY 4

Exercise for today
Jump Rope
Color the star when you complete each level.

☆ 1-5 Reps
☆ 6-10 Reps
☆ 10-20 Reps

WEEK 4

Geometry

1. Trace the name of this shape.    Rectangle

2. How many sides? _____ How many vertexes (corners)? _____

3. Trace and draw the Rectangle.

   _____ _____

DAY 4

4. Finish the pattern.

   _____ _____ _____

Self-discipline is to have control of your actions.

Photo courtesy of Stephanie Lopez Cox

Stephanie Lopez Cox works hard to reach her goals. Her focus and dedication helped her earn a spot on the US National Women's Soccer Team that won a gold medal in the Olympics. Stephanie practices very hard and is committed to being the best athlete that she can be and is dedicated to bettering the world around her.

Self-discipline means self-control. Make good choices.

Noah's mom said he could have 2 cookies after he did his homework.

Show Noah having self-discipline and draw how many cookies his mom said he could have.

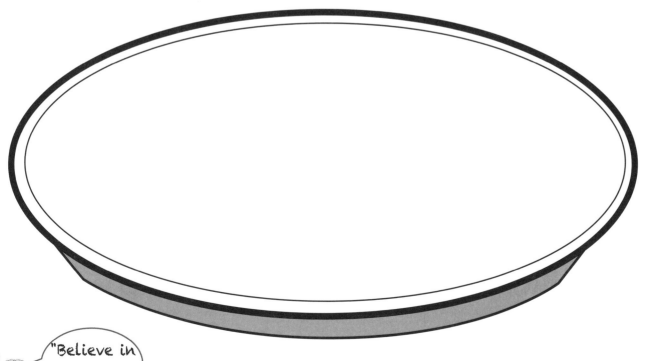

"Believe in yourself!"

Choose 1 or more activities to do with your family or friends. Color today's star when you are finished. Good job!

☐ Clean up after yourself without being asked. Work hard to remember to put away your things. Ask a parent or guardian to help you make a job chart. Put a sticker on the chart each time you do a chore.

☐ Make a mosaic out of cut up paper or tissue paper. Practice self-discipline by cutting and gluing all the pieces.

☐ Ask a parent or guardian to help you make an "anger box." Fill a small box with things that will help you calm down and get control when you are angry (bubbles, playdough, small bouncy ball, paper and crayons).

Core Value Book List
Read More About Self-Discipline

The Story About Ping
By Marjorie Flack

Messy
By Barbara Bottner

The Grouch Ladybug
By Eric Carle

Reading Extension Activities at SummerFitLearning.com

Let's Talk About It

Help your child understand that there are consequences to their good and bad behavior. Role play ways to show self-discipline in different situations. Encourage your child to walk away and calm down when they are frustrated rather than have an outburst.

Play Time!
Choose a Game or Activity to Play for 60 minutes today!

YOU CHOOSE

_____

Write down which game or activity you played today!

Be Healthy! Turn off the TV when you eat.

Watch exercise videos at www.summerfitlearning.com

WEEK 5

PARENT GUIDE WEEK 5

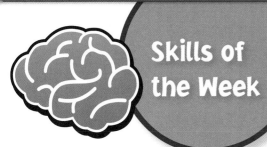

Skills of the Week

✔ Healthy choices
✔ Addition
✔ Poetry
✔ Subtraction
✔ Colors
✔ Seasons
✔ Dozen
✔ Short o
✔ Long o
✔ Pentagons

Kindness

Princess Diana

Kindness is caring about people, animals and the earth. It is looking for ways to help others.

Being nice to others catches on. When people are nice to each other they feel better about themselves and others. Small things make a big difference so when you smile, lend a helping hand and show concern for others, you are making the world a better place.

Play Every Day!

Weekly Extension Activities at SummerFitLearning.com

Kindness In Action!

Color the star each day you show kindness through your own actions.

WEEK 5

Color the ⭐ As You Complete Your Daily Task

	Day 1	Day 2	Day 3	Day 4	Day 5
MIND	⭐	⭐	⭐	⭐	⭐
BODY	⭐	⭐	⭐	⭐	⭐
DAILY READING	⭐ 20 minutes	⭐ 20 minutes	⭐ 20 minutes	⭐ 20 minutes	⭐ 20 minutes

"You Can do It"

"I am kind"

_____
Print Name

I can make good choices and eat healthy food that will help my brain and body grow. Circle the pictures of healthy food.

Exercise for today
Dancing Shoes
Color the star when you complete each level.

☆ 10-30 Seconds
☆ 31-60 Seconds
☆ 61-90 Seconds

Be Healthy!
Tell your family what made you feel happy today.

Addition

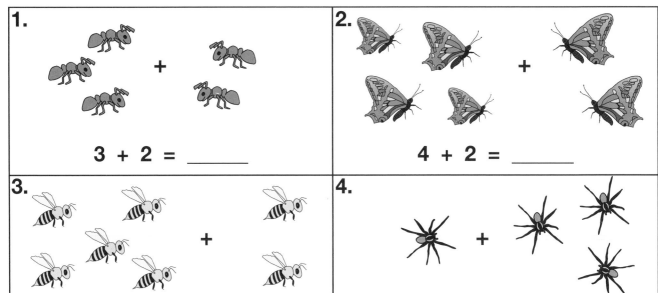

1.

3 + 2 = _____

2.

4 + 2 = _____

3.

5 + 2 = _____

4.

1 + 3 = _____

5. Spiders are not insects they are arachnids.
Spiders have 8 legs. Draw the legs on the spider and color.

Read the poem or have your parent read it to you. Draw a picture showing what the poem is about.

Caterpillar
-Christina Rossetti

Brown and furry
Caterpillar in a hurry,
Take your walk
To the shady leaf, or stalk,
Or what not,

Which may be the chosen spot.
No toad spy you,
Hovering bird of prey pass by you,
Spin and die,
To live again a butterfly.

Strength

 Go to www.summerfitlearning.com for more Activities!

Exercise for today
Bear Crawl
Color the star when you complete each level.

☆ **1-5 Reps**
☆ **6-10 Reps**
☆ **10-20 Reps**

Be Healthy!
Share a joke with a friend.

WEEK 5

DAY 2

 **Numbers and Math - Gumball math**

Follow the directions to color the gum balls.

Color 6 in red
Color 5 in yellow
Color 3 in green
Color 8 in blue
Color 2 in pink

_____

1. How many more red gumballs than yellow?

6 - 5 = _____

_____

2. How many more blue gum balls than red?

8 – 6 = _____

_____

3. How many gum balls in all?

_____

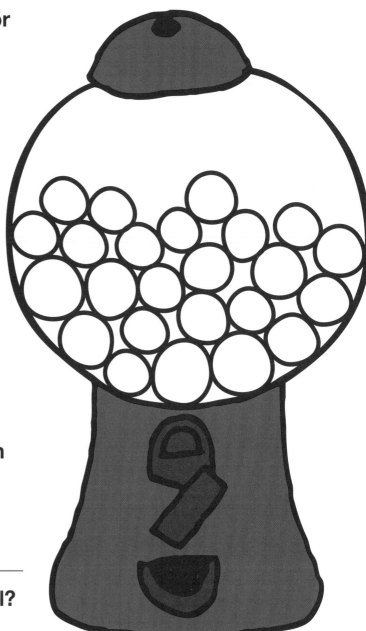

Trace the names of the 4 seasons. Circle what you might use in each season.

1.

winter

2.

spring

3.

summer

4.

fall

WEEK 5

DAY 3

Aerobic Go to www.summerfitlearning.com for more Activities!

Exercise for today	
Run or Jog	☆ **10-30 Seconds**
Color the star when you complete each level.	☆ 31-60 Seconds
	☆ **61-90 Seconds**

Be Healthy!
Quench your thirst with water or milk.

Math - Mixed Practice

1. Count how many cupcakes.

_____

2. 12 of something is a dozen. Circle the objects that have a dozen.

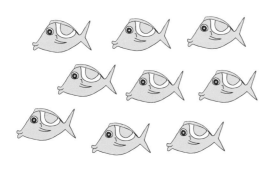

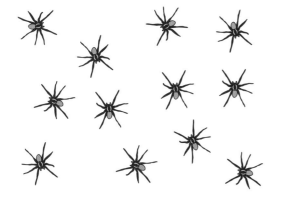

WEEK 5

DAY 3

Draw a line to find rhyming words with the short o sound.

Circle the pictures with the long o sound as in (boat)

YELLOW

WEEK 5

DAY 4

Strength
Go to www.summerfitlearning.com for more Activities!

Exercise for today
Hula-Hoop
Color the star when you complete each level.

☆ 1-5 Reps
☆ 6-10 Reps
☆ 10-20 Reps

Be Healthy!
Smile ☺

WEEK 5

DAY 4

 Geometry

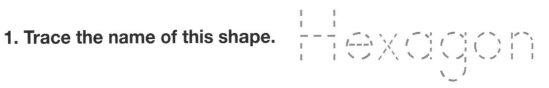

1. **Trace the name of this shape.**

Hexagon

2. **How many sides?** _____ **How many vertexes (corners)?** _____

3. **Trace and draw the hexagon.**

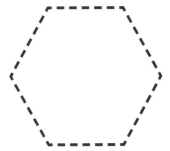

_____   _____

4. **What comes next? Color the patterns.**

○ □ △ ○ □ _____

□ ○ □ ○ □ _____

⬡ ⬡ ⬡ ⬡ ⬡ _____

74 © Summer Fit

Kindness is being nice and caring about people, animals, and the earth.

Princess Diana

Princess Diana was a kind princess who cared for people who felt alone and forgotten. She made ordinary people feel very special by visiting and listening to them. Princess Diana had a big heart and was kind to everyone.

Sharing your toys is a way of being kind.

Draw a picture of yourself sharing your toys.

"Sharing my toys makes me feel good!"

"Believe in yourself!"

Choose 1 or more activities to do with your family or friends. Color today's star when you are finished. Good job!

☐ Cut out a heart badge that says "Kindness starts with me." Spread kindness wherever you go this week by saying kind words and doing kind acts.

☐ Collect coins to give to a homeless shelter or Habitat for Humanity.

☐ Help your mom around the house. Offer to help make dinner or set the table.

Core Value Book List
Read More About Kindness

A Circle of Friends
By Giora Carmi

How Kind!
By Mary Murphy

I Likie Your Buttons
By Sarah Lamstein

Reading Extension Activities at SummerFitLearning.com

 ### Let's Talk About It

Children learn what they live, so if they live with you doing random acts of kindness, they'll most certainly follow. Discuss the many little ways they can show kindness to others each day. Teach them that kindness comes in all shapes and sizes and it's free.

Play Time!
Choose a Game or Activity to Play for 60 minutes today!

YOU CHOOSE

_____

Write down which game or activity you played today!

Watch exercise videos at www.summerfitlearning.com

Be Healthy! Have fruit with breakfast.

WEEK 6

Skills of the Week

✔ Map skills
✔ Directions
✔ Number words
✔ Beginning letters
✔ Sorting sets
✔ Count by 10's
✔ Addition
✔ Subtraction
✔ Sight words
✔ Mixed practice
✔ Rhyming words
✔ Lines of symmetry

Courage

Rosa Parks

Courage means doing the right thing even when it is difficult and you are afraid. It means to be brave.

It can be a lot easier to do the right thing when everybody else is doing it, but it can be a lot harder to do it on your own or when nobody is looking. Remember who you are and stand up for what you believe in when it is easy and even more so when it is hard.

Play Every Day!

Weekly Extension Activities at SummerFitLearning.com

Courage In Action!
Color the star each day you show Courage through your own actions.

WEEK 6

Color the ⭐ As You Complete Your Daily Task

	Day 1	Day 2	Day 3	Day 4	Day 5
MIND	⭐	⭐	⭐	⭐	⭐
BODY	⭐	⭐	⭐	⭐	⭐
DAILY READING	⭐ 20 minutes	⭐ 20 minutes	⭐ 20 minutes	⭐ 20 minutes	⭐ 20 minutes

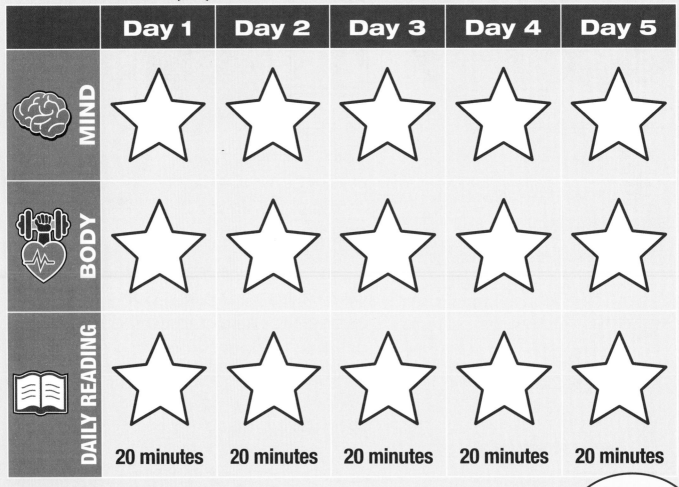

"You Can do It"

"I am brave"

Print Name

Geography - On the Map

Courage

North, South, East, West are directions.

Here is a map of a farmyard. Look at the directions to find each object on the map below.

WEEK 6

1. The  is _____

2. The  is _____

3. The  is _____

4. The  is _____

DAY 1

Aerobic
Go to www.summerfitlearning.com for more Activities!

Be Healthy!
Eat an apple!

Exercise for today
Ghost Run or Jog
Color the star when you complete each level.

☆ 10-30 Seconds
☆ 31-60 Seconds
☆ 61-90 Seconds

WEEK 6

DAY 1

 Number words

Match each numeral to the correct number word.

1	five
2	nine
3	six
4	seven
5	one
6	eight
7	ten
8	three
9	two
10	four

Write the letter of each beginning sound on the line.

1.
_ _ _ _ _ _

2.
_ _ _ _ _ _

3.
_ _ _ _ _ _

4.
_ _ _ _ _ _

5.
_ _ _ _ _ _

6.
_ _ _ _ _ _

7.
_ _ _ _ _ _

8.
_ _ _ _ _ _

9.
_ _ _ _ _ _

10.
_ _ _ _ _ _

11.
_ _ _ _ _ _

12
_ _ _ _ _ _

13.
_ _ _ _ _ _

14.
_ _ _ _ _ _

15.
_ _ _ _ _ _

16
_ _ _ _ _ _

Strength

Exercise for today
Crab Crawl
Color the star when you complete each level.

 1-5 Reps
 6-10 Reps
 10-20 Reps

Be Healthy!
Fresh fruits come from your garden or a farm.

WEEK 6

DAY 2

 Math - Sort the Sets

1. How many cats? _____   2. How many dogs? _____

3. How many cats and dogs together?_____

_____ + _____ = _____

4. How many more dogs than cats? _____

_____ - _____ = _____

5. Count by 10's

10, 20, _____, _____, _____, _____, _____, _____, _____, 100

Help Felix the frog read his way across the pond to his mother.
Color the lily pad of each word you can read.

Aerobic

Go to www.summerfitlearning.com for more Activities!

Exercise for today
Ball/Frisbee Toss and Run
Color the star when you complete each level.

☆ **10-30 Seconds**
☆ 31-60 Seconds
☆ **61-90 Seconds**

Be Healthy!
Walnuts look like a brain- they make you smart!

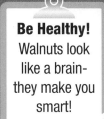

WEEK 6

DAY 3

`1+2=3` `+` `−` `×` `÷` `=` **Math - Mixed Practice**

Count backwards from 20 to 1.

1. 20, ____, ____, ____, ____, ____, ____,13, ____, ____

2. 10, ____, ____, ____, 6, ____, ____, ____, ____, ____

Color the tallest tree green	Color the shortest flower red
3. 	4.

Circle one.

In	Out
5. 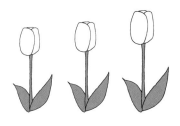	6.

7. Write the sums.

Ex: 4 + 2 = ___6___   2 + 2 = _____   3 + 3 = _____   5 + 1 = _____

© Summer Fit

"Rhyme time"

Circle the words in each row that rhyme.

1. cat	hat	pig	mat
2. frog	sun	dog	hog
3. run	man	sun	fun
4. pop	top	rip	hop
5. fish	tip	dish	wish
6. car	pot	star	far

WEEK 6

DAY 4

Exercise for today
Rowboat

Color the star when you complete each level.

☆ **1-5 Reps**
☆ **6-10 Reps**
☆ **10-20 Reps**

Geometry, lines of symmetry

Add the other half of each shape to make it whole.

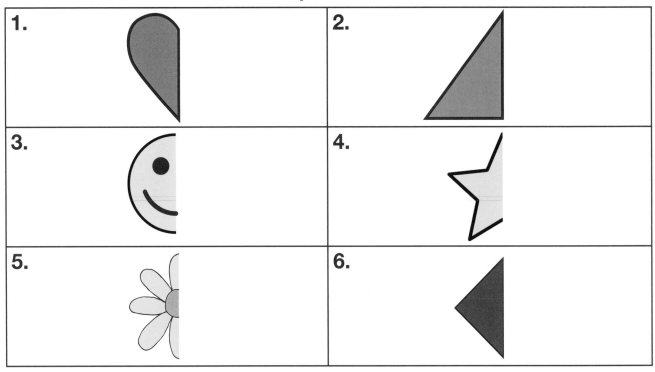

1.

2.

3.

4.

5.

6.

Finish each pattern. Color.

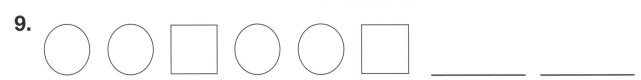

7. ▢ ○ ▢ ○ _____ _____

8. ◇ △ ◇ △ _____ _____

9. ○ ○ ▢ ○ ○ ▢ _____ _____

WEEK 6

DAY 4

Courage means doing the right thing even when you are feeling scared.

Rosa Parks

Rosa Parks believed that all people should be treated equally no matter the color of their skin. When she was young, black people had to give up their seats to white people when they were on a bus. Even though she was afraid, one day she refused to give up her seat. Many people were proud of Rosa Parks and it showed them that they too should stand up for what is right. Her act of courage helped change the law so that all people could be treated equally.

I can show courage every day by being brave.

Draw a picture of yourself being brave.

"Believe in yourself!"

Choose 1 or more activities to do with your family or friends. Color today's star when you are finished. Good job!

- ☐ Draw 3 things that make you afraid. Talk to your parents about how you can overcome these fears.
- ☐ Try a new food.
- ☐ Speak up for someone who is being teased. Offer to be their friend.
- ☐ Try a new game or sport.

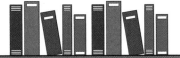

Core Value Book List
Read More About Courage

The Brave Little Bird
By Scott Beck

Rainbow Fish to the Rescue
By Marcus Pfister

There's a Monster Under my Bed
By James Howe

Reading Extension Activities at SummerFitLearning.com

Let's Talk About It

Talk about what it means to be courageous. Role play different opportunities your child has to be brave. Talk about ways to handle situations like fears, teasing, bullying. Catch your child being brave and praise them for their courage.

Stepping Stones

Stepping Stones Entertainment™ was founded by parents who wanted to provide meaningful family movies to help inspire common values. It is made up of people from many different backgrounds, nationalities and beliefs. For more than 20 years, Stepping Stones has provided families with movies about integrity, charity, forgiveness and many other common values through hundreds of films for all ages. Learn more at **www.steppingstones.com**.

STEPPING STONES.com
Meaningful Family Movies

Play Time!
Choose a Game or Activity to Play for 60 minutes today!

YOU CHOOSE

_____
Write down which game or activity you played today!

Be Healthy!
Name a fruit or vegetable that is green.

Watch exercise videos at www.summerfitlearning.com

PARENT GUIDE WEEK 7

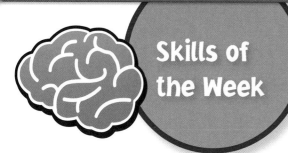

Skills of the Week

Respect

Mahatma Gandhi

- ✔ Consonant blends
- ✔ Making a ten
- ✔ Place value
- ✔ Vowels
- ✔ Calendar
- ✔ Beginning blends
- ✔ Less and more
- ✔ Time
- ✔ Money
- ✔ Parts of a flower
- ✔ Shapes

Respect is honoring yourself and others. It is behaving in a way that makes life peaceful and orderly.

Sometimes we forget to appreciate that every person is unique and different. All of us want to be accepted and appreciated for who we are. Try to treat others the way that you want to be treated, even when it is difficult.

Play Every Day!

GET FIT TIME!

Weekly Extension Activities at SummerFitLearning.com

Respect In Action!
Color the star each day you show respect through your own actions.

WEEK 7
HEALTHY MIND + HEALTHY BODY

Color the ⭐ As You Complete Your Daily Task

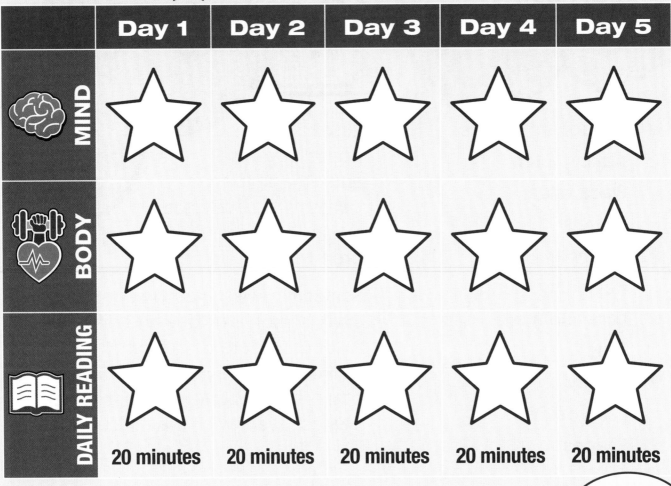

	Day 1	Day 2	Day 3	Day 4	Day 5
MIND	⭐	⭐	⭐	⭐	⭐
BODY	⭐	⭐	⭐	⭐	⭐
DAILY READING	⭐ 20 minutes	⭐ 20 minutes	⭐ 20 minutes	⭐ 20 minutes	⭐ 20 minutes

"I am respectful"

"You Can do It"

Print Name

Circle the pictures in each row that begin with the blend shown.

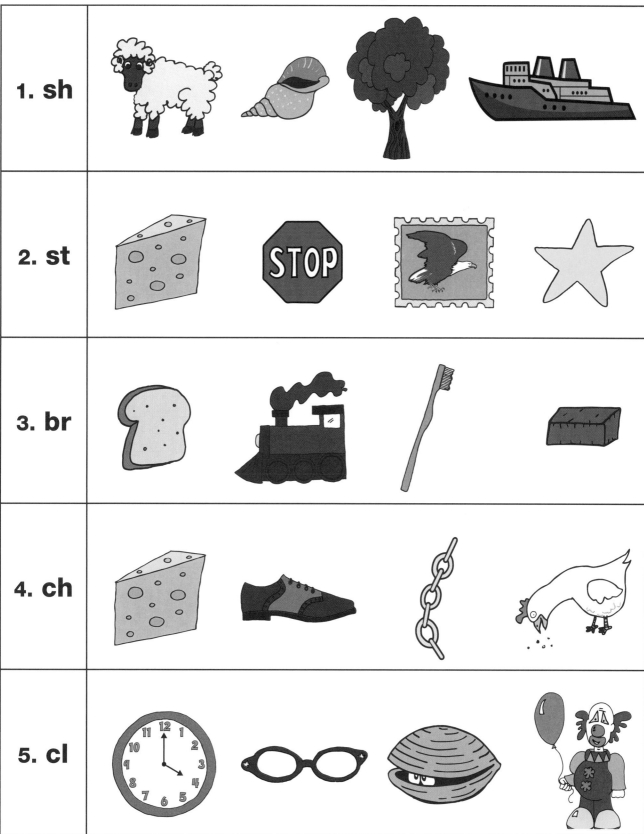

1. sh				
2. st				
3. br				
4. ch				
5. cl				

Aerobic

Go to www.summerfitlearning.com for more Activities!

Exercise for today
Freeze Tag
Color the star when you complete each level.

☆ **10-30 Seconds**
☆ 31-60 Seconds
☆ **61-90 Seconds**

Be Healthy!
Each color vegetable gives you a different power to be healthy!

WEEK 7

DAY 1

Math - Make a Ten ★★★★★★★★★★★★★

1.

 _____ |  _____

 _____ |  _____

 _____ |  _____

 _____ | _____

 _____ |  _____

2. Underline the digit in the ones place.

1<u>3</u>	27	18	60	33	49
ex					

3. Circle the digit in the tens place.

(1)0	15	22	38	40	25
ex					

a e i o u

Write the vowel to complete each word. Color the pictures.

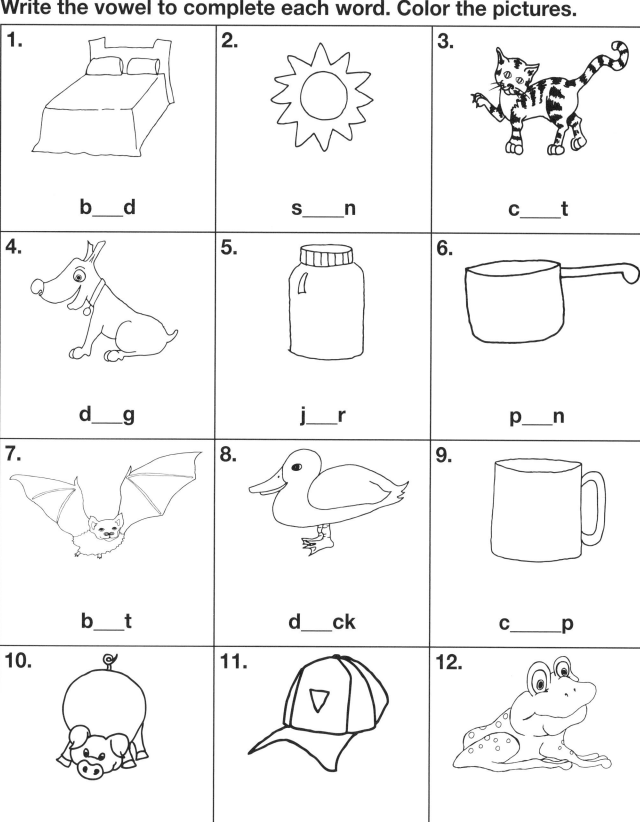

1.

b___d

2.

s____n

3.

c____t

4.

d___g

5.

j___r

6.

p___n

7.

b___t

8.

d___ck

9.

c____p

10.

p___g

11.

h___t

12.

fr___g

WEEK 7

DAY 2

Strength

 Go to www.summerfitlearning.com for more Activities!

Exercise for today
Freeze Dance
Color the star when you complete each level.

☆ **1-5 Reps**
☆ **6-10 Reps**
☆ **10-20 Reps**

Be Healthy!
Fresh vegetables come from your garden or a farm.

 Calendar Days

sunny   cloudy   rainy

Look at the calendar. Answer the questions.

MAY

		1 ☀	2 ☀	3 ☀	4 ☀	5 🌧
6 🌧	7 ☁	8 ☁	9 ☁	10 🌧	11 ☀	12 ☀
13 ☀	14 ☀	15 ☀	16 ☀	17 ☀	18 ☀	19 ☀
20 🌧	21 🌧	22 ☁	23 ☁	24 ☀	25 ☀	26 ☀
27 ☁	28 🌧	29 🌧	30 ☁	31 ☀		

1. How many days were sunny? _____

2. How many days were rainy? _____

3. How many days were cloudy? _____

4. How many days in the month of May? _____

_____

_ _ _ _ _ _ _ _ _ _ _ _ _ _ _ _ _ _ _ _

5. What kind of weather was it most days? _____

94 © Summer Fit

Circle the beginning blend for each picture.

1. sh cl ch	2. sn sl th	3. pl tr fr
4. sk fr sl	**5. pl wh cr**	**6. ch sm th**
7. tr wh th	**8. pl gl st**	**9. wh sk sn**
10. br sl pl	**11. sl sn cr**	**12. fr bl cl**

Go to www.summerfitlearning.com for more Activities!

Aerobic

Exercise for today
Egg Race
Color the star when you complete each level.

☆ **10-30 Seconds**
☆ **31-60 Seconds**
☆ **61-90 Seconds**

Be Healthy!
Make popsicles out of your favorite fruit juice!

Numbers and Math - Mixed Practice

1. Draw a line to match the clock to the time.

   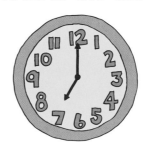   

12:00   3:00   7:00

2. Count the penguins. Circle the 8th penguin from the left.

_____ penguins

3. Circle the number that is less

12 10	18 20	25 27	10 15

4. What is the value of a:

_____¢   _____¢   _____¢

Flowers come in all sizes, shapes and colors. But all flowers have the same job, to make seeds that will grow into new plants.

The parts of the flower are the petals, seeds, stem, leaf, and roots.

Label the parts of the flower. Color the flower.

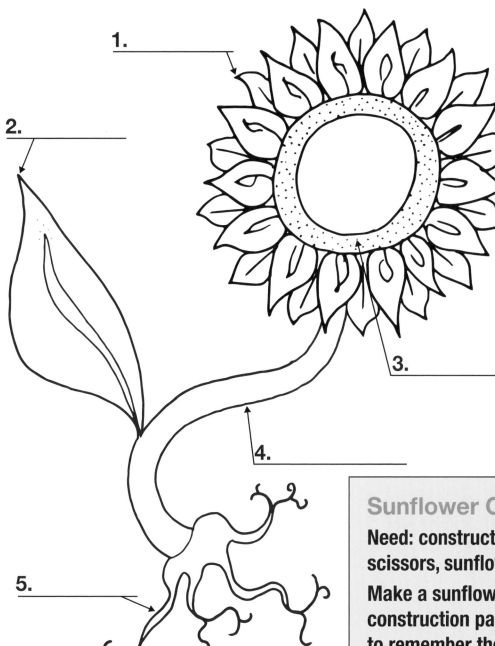

1. _____

2. _____

3. _____

4. _____

5. _____

Sunflower Craft

Need: construction paper, glue, scissors, sunflower seeds.

Make a sunflower out of construction paper, make sure to remember the stem and leaves. Glue sunflower seed to center of the flower, just like a real sunflower.

Strength

Go to www.summerfitlearning.com for more Activities!

Exercise for today
Snake Curl

Color the star when you complete each level.

☆ 1-5 Reps
☆ 6-10 Reps
☆ 10-20 Reps

Be Healthy!
Cook a meal with your family today.

 Geometry - Sort and count the shapes

Count the shapes. Color as directed.
Color Key:
Blue square
Yellow triangle
Red rectangle
Green circle
Orange hexagon

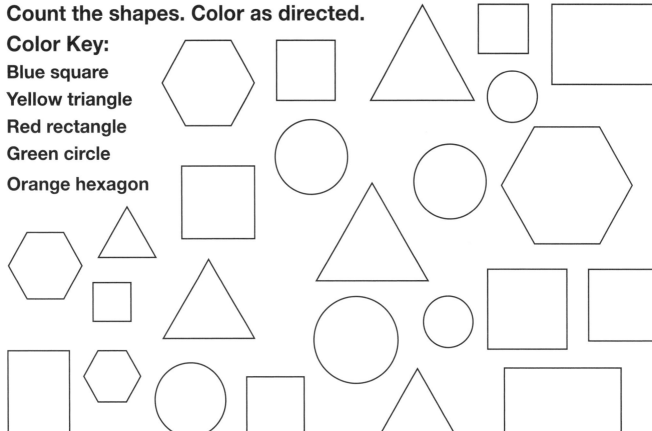

1. How many ▲? _____

2. How many ● ? _____

3. How many ■ ? _____

4. How many ■ ? _____

5. How many ⬡ ? _____

6. How many shapes all together? _____

WEEK 7

DAY 4

98 © Summer Fit

Respect is being nice to yourself and to others.

Mahatma Gandhi

Mahatma Gandhi was one of the greatest leaders the world has ever known. Gandhi taught that if you hurt someone else you were also hurting yourself. He believed in peace and getting along rather than fighting. Gandhi wanted everyone to get along and believed there would be peace in the world if everyone would love and respect each other.

The things that make me "me" are the things that make me special.

We are all different and special in our own way. Draw hair, eyes, a nose and mouth to look like you. Then answer the questions about yourself.

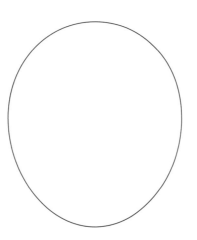

My favorite food is:_____   My favorite color is: _____

I like: _____   I don't like: _____

I am good at: _____

"Believe in yourself!"

Choose 1 or more activities to do with your family or friends. Color today's star when you are finished. Good job!

☐ Play a game of Simon Says but make sure to say the words: "Simon says please…"

☐ Have a family meeting and decide what rules are most important to your family. Write them down and post them where everyone can see.

☐ Pick a country to study. Learn about the land, people, and customs. Make and sample a food you normally don't eat.

☐ Make an "I am a star" poster. On it put pictures and facts about all the things that make you special and unique.

Core Value Book List
Read More About Respect

Arthur's Eyes
By Marc Brown

Sister Anne's Hands
By Marybeth Lorbiecki

Yoko
By Rosemary Wells

Reading Extension Activities at SummerFitLearning.com

 ### Let's Talk About It

There are many ways for people to show respect to others, and the more children understand what those ways are, the more likely they are to incorporate them into their daily lives. Make sure to point out that people must respect themselves before they are able to respect others.

 # Play Time!
Choose a Game or Activity to Play for 60 minutes today!

YOU CHOOSE

_____

Write down which game or activity you played today!

Watch exercise videos at www.summerfitlearning.com

 **Be Healthy!** Wash your hands.

WEEK 8

Skills of the Week

Responsibility

Terry Fox

✔ My body
✔ Following directions
✔ Sums and differences
✔ Money
✔ Double ee
✔ Syllables
✔ Tally marks
✔ Ordering
✔ Tens and ones
✔ Spider storytelling
✔ Shapes

Being responsible means others can depend on you. It is being accountable for what you do and for what you do not do.

A lot of times it is easier to look to someone else to step forward and do the work or to blame others when it does not get done. You are smart, capable and able so try to be the person who accepts challenges and does not blame others if it does not get done.

Play Every Day!

Weekly Extension Activities at SummerFitLearning.com

Responsibility In Action!
Color the star each day you show responsibility through your own actions.

WEEK 8

Color the ⭐ As You Complete Your Daily Task

	Day 1	Day 2	Day 3	Day 4	Day 5
MIND	☆	☆	☆	☆	☆
BODY	☆	☆	☆	☆	☆
DAILY READING	☆	☆	☆	☆	☆
	20 minutes	20 minutes	20 minutes	20 minutes	20 minutes

"You Can do It"

"I am responsible"

_____
Print Name

Draw a line from each word to its correct body part.

head   hair

eyes   nose

mouth   neck

shoulder   arm

hand   wrist

chest   stomach

leg   knee

ankle   foot

WEEK 8

DAY 1

WEEK 8

DAY 1

Exercise for today	
Swimming Scissors	

Color the star when you complete each level.

☆ **10-30 Seconds**
☆ 31-60 Seconds
☆ **61-90 Seconds**

Be Healthy!
Instead of juice, mix a piece of fruit with water.

 Following Directions

1. Circle the hand on the left.   2. Underline the foot on the right.

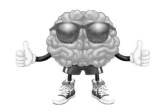   

Finish the sums and differences.

3. Ex: 7 + 3 = __10__   4. 10 − 3 = ____   5. 10 − 5 = ____   6. 5 + 5 = ____

 = 10 cents   = 5 cents   = 1 cent

7.   = _____ ¢

8.    = _____ ¢

9.   = _____ ¢

Letters and Sounds - Double ee

Responsibility

Fill in the double ee to finish these long e words.

1. J ___ ___ p

2. wh ___ ___ l

3. h ___ ___ l

4. qu ___ ___ n

5. sh ___ ___ p

6. f ___ ___ t

Read the words. Clap out the syllables with your hands. Write the number on the line.

7. apple _____

8. banana _____

9. grapes _____

10. orange _____

WEEK 8

DAY 2

Strength
Go to www.summerfitlearning.com for more Activities!

Exercise for today
Chair Leg-lifts
Color the star when you complete each level.

☆ **1-5 Reps**
☆ **6-10 Reps**
☆ **10-20 Reps**

Be Healthy!
Instead of a sweet, try toast with cream cheese or peanut butter!

WEEK 8

DAY 2

1+2=3
➕➖
✖➗＝
Math - Tally Marks

Look at the chart of tally marks for the class pets.
Count the tally marks and write the number of each pet.

1.	ЖЖ	_____
2.	ЖЖ II	_____
3.	III	_____
4.	II	_____
5.	I	_____

6. What is the pet with the most tally marks? _____

7. What is the pet with the least? _____

8. How many pets all together in this class? _____

9. Write tally marks to tell your age. _____

© Summer Fit

1. How does a plant grow? Seeds need many things to grow into a healthy plant. Number the steps 1-6 in order for a seed to grow.

2. What happens next?

Number the pictures in the order of how they should happen.

WEEK 8

DAY 3

WEEK 8

Exercise for today
Stepping Up
Color the star when you complete each level.

☆ **10-30 Seconds**
☆ **31-60 Seconds**
☆ **61-90 Seconds**

Be Healthy!
Instead of potato chips, try POPCORN!

 Number Practice

How many tens and ones?

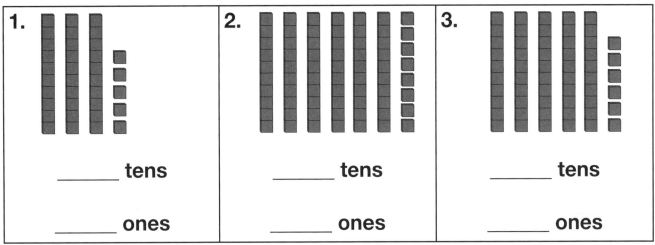

1.
_____ tens

_____ ones

2.
_____ tens

_____ ones

3.
_____ tens

_____ ones

4. Using 2 colors, color the blocks to show 2 different ways to make 6.

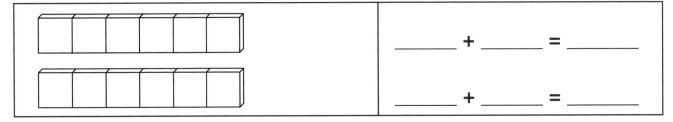

_____ + _____ = _____

_____ + _____ = _____

5. Draw a dozen eggs in the nest.

6. Draw a pair of shoes.

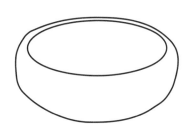

DAY 3

You look down and see a spider crawling near your foot.

Think of 4 words to describe the spider. Words that describe are called adjectives.

_____   _____

_____   _____

Write a sentence or two to tell a spider story using the words above. Illustrate your story.

_____

_____

_____

_____

_____

Exercise for today
Giraffe Walk
Color the star when you complete each level.

☆ 1-5 Reps
☆ 6-10 Reps
☆ 10-20 Reps

Be Healthy!
Take a walk with your parents today.

 Geometry

1. Color the shapes with more than 3 sides.

   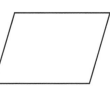

2. Color the shapes with 4 vertices (corners).

   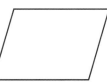

3. Color half the shape

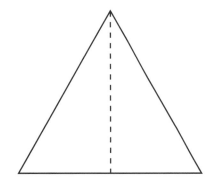

4. Color half the shape.

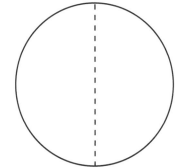

WEEK 8

DAY 4

© Photo courtesy of the Terry Fox Foundation

www.terryfox.org

Responsibility is to do the things you know that you should.

Terrance Stanley Fox

Terrance Stanley Fox was a very good athlete. Sadly, he got cancer and because of that he lost one of his legs. Once he got an artificial leg, he set off to run across Canada and raise money for cancer research. Terry felt it was his responsibility to do all that he could for other people with cancer. When he started to run not many people knew about Terry or what he was doing but now people all over the world participate or take part in an event named after Terry to raise money for cancer research.

Draw a picture of something you are responsible for. For example: taking care of a pet, cleaning your room.

"Believe in yourself!"

Choose 1 or more activities to do with your family or friends. Color today's star when you are finished. Good job!

☐ Plant a garden and be responsible for weeding and watering it.

Core Value Book List
Read More About Responsibility

The Little Red Lighthouse and the Great Gray Bridge
By Hildegarde Swift

I'll Tell on You
By Joan Lexau

Keep the Lights Burning Abbie
By Connie and Peter Roop

Reading Extension Activities at SummerFitLearning.com

☐ What chores are you responsible for at home? Have your parents help you make a chore chart to keep track of them. Be responsible and do your chores without being told.

☐ Think about the words you say. Can your words hurt people? Think of someone you may have hurt with your words. Make them a card to say you are sorry.

Let's Talk About It

Responsibility can be taught through simple, daily ways. Being responsible is an attitude as much as a skill. Children are able to do chores starting at a young age. Give them age-appropriate tasks and hold them responsible to complete them. Point out to them once they complete their tasks how "responsible" they were in completing them and positively reinforce their actions.

Play Time!
Choose a Game or Activity to Play for 60 minutes today!

YOU CHOOSE

_____
Write down which game or activity you played today!

Watch exercise videos at www.summerfitlearning.com

Be Healthy!
Plant a family garden and eat what you grow.

WEEK 9

Skills of the Week

- ✔ Long a
- ✔ Ordering
- ✔ Long i
- ✔ Days of the week
- ✔ Long u
- ✔ Measurement
- ✔ Before and after numbers
- ✔ Insects
- ✔ 3D shapes

Perseverance

Bethany Hamilton

Perseverance means not giving up or giving in when things are difficult. It means you try again when you fail.

Sometimes it is easy to forget that a lot of things in life require patience and hard work. Do not give up because it is hard to accomplish a task or to get something that we want. Focus on your goal and keep working hard. It is through this experience that you will accomplish what you want.

GET FIT TIME!

Play Every Day!

Weekly Extension Activities at SummerFitLearning.com

Perseverance In Action!

Color the star each day you show perseverance through your own actions.

Color the ⭐ As You Complete Your Daily Task

	Day 1	Day 2	Day 3	Day 4	Day 5
MIND	⭐	⭐	⭐	⭐	⭐
BODY	⭐	⭐	⭐	⭐	⭐
DAILY READING	⭐	⭐	⭐	⭐	⭐
	20 minutes	20 minutes	20 minutes	20 minutes	20 minutes

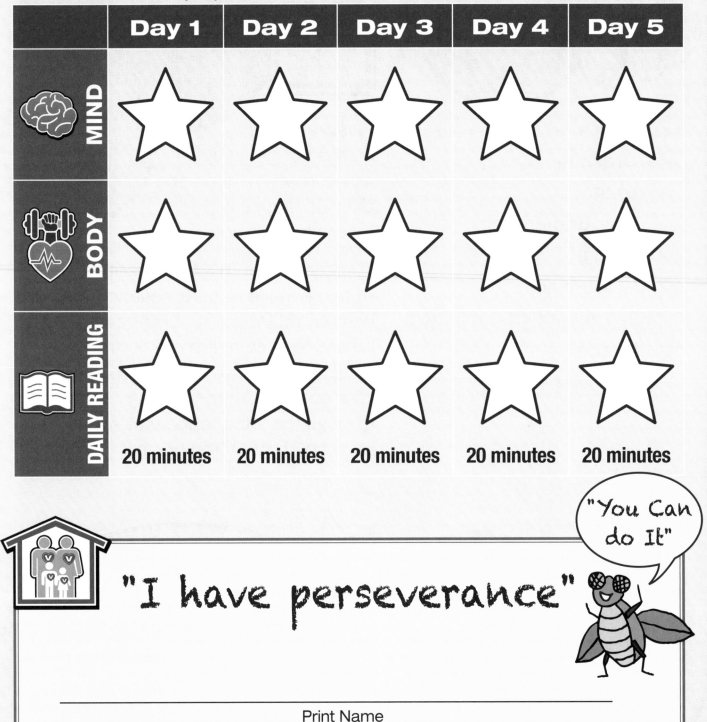

"You Can do It"

"I have perseverance"

Print Name

Ape has the long a sound.

Color the pictures that have a long a sound.

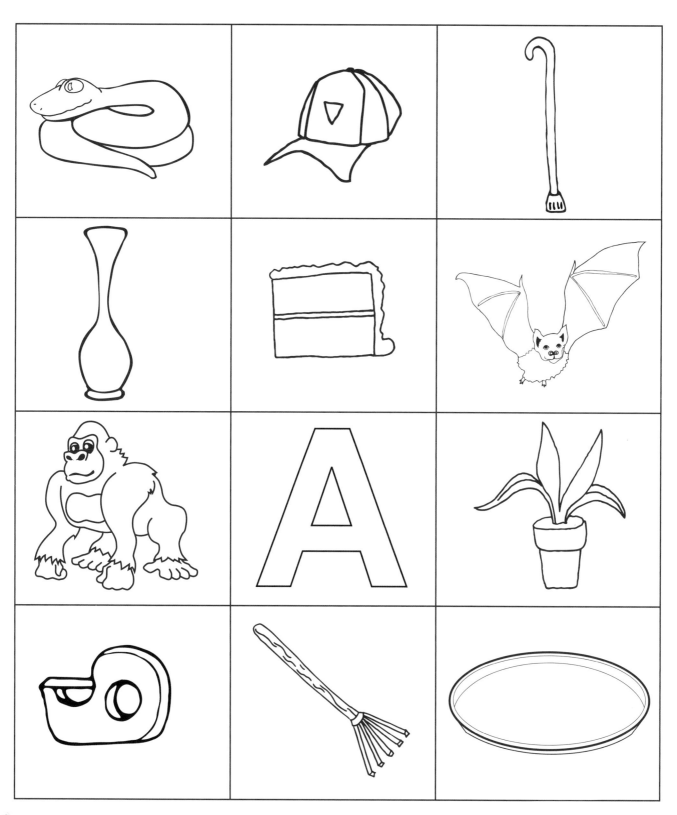

Aerobic

Go to www.summerfitlearning.com for more Activities!

Exercise for today
Hill Run or Jog
Color the star when you complete each level.

☆ 10-30 Seconds
☆ 31-60 Seconds
☆ 61-90 Seconds

Be Healthy!
Try a new food today.

Numbers and Math

---

1. Circle the 9ᵗʰ apple

---

2. Circle the 5ᵗʰ star

---

3. Circle the 7ᵗʰ banana

---

4. Circle the 3ʳᵈ spider

---

5. Circle the 10ᵗʰ triangle

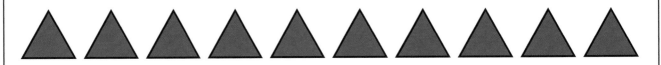

WEEK 9

DAY 1

Kite has the long i sound.

Circle all the pictures with the long i sound.

WEEK 9

DAY 2

Exercise for today
Bunny Bounce
Color the star when you complete each level.

☆ **1-5 Reps**
☆ **6-10 Reps**
☆ **10-20 Reps**

Math - Counting Practice

Count the days of the week.

1.

Sunday _____

Monday _____

Tuesday _____

Wednesday _____

Thursday _____

Friday _____

Saturday _____

2. Circle the 2nd day.

3. Underline the fifth day.

4. How many days begin with T? _____

5. How many days begin with S? _____

Count the coins. Write the value of each set.

2. _____ ¢

3. _____ ¢

4. _____ ¢

WEEK 9

DAY 2

"Long u words" Circle the 8 words that have the long u sound as in  cube.

BLUE

Aerobic

Go to www.summerfitlearning.com for more Activities!

Exercise for today
Hi Yah
Color the star when you complete each level.

☆ 10-30 Seconds
☆ 31-60 Seconds
☆ 61-90 Seconds

Be Healthy!
Eat your snack at the table, not in front of the computer or television.

WEEK 9

DAY 3

Math - Measurement

1.

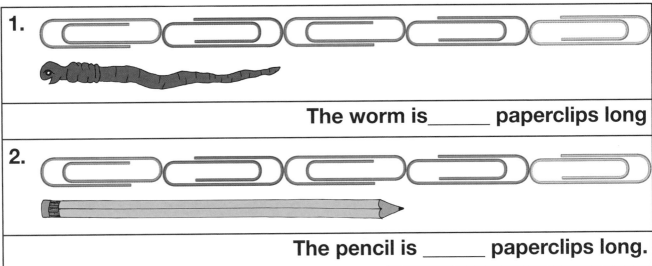

The worm is_____ paperclips long

2.

The pencil is _____ paperclips long.

3. Circle the mouse that is behind the cheese.

4. Circle the peanuts inside the jar.

5. Circle the spider that is under the leaf.

120 © Summer Fit

An insect has 3 body parts. It has a hard outer skeleton and 6 legs. An insect has antennae (an-ten'-ee) on its head and most insects have 2 pairs of wings.

Draw a line from each picture of an insect to its name, then color the insects.

1.    caterpillar

2.    fly

3.    beetle

4. 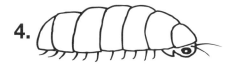   ladybug

5. 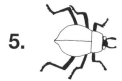   bee

6.    butterfly

7.    grasshopper

8.    ant

Strength

Go to www.summerfitlearning.com for more Activities!

Exercise for today
Crab Kick

Color the star when you complete each level.

☆ **1-5 Reps**
☆ **6-10 Reps**
☆ **10-20 Reps**

Be Healthy!
Farmer's Market sells local produce.

WEEK 9

Shapes

1. Write the name of the shape you see in each picture.

◯	▢	△	▭
Circle	square	triangle	rectangle

Circle   _____   _____   _____

"3D Shapes"

2. **Circle the name of this shape.**

       pyramid   **sphere**

3. The name of this shape **is a....**

       cone   **cube**

4. Circle the name of this 3D shape **.**

       sphere   **cylinder**

DAY 4

122 © Summer Fit

Perseverance is trying again and again and not giving up.

Bethany Hamilton

Bethany Hamilton was sitting on her surfboard when suddenly a shark attacked, sadly she lost her arm. When Bethany got better, she decided to surf again even though she was scared. She had to learn how to surf with only one arm and even though it was hard, she persevered and never gave up.

Spoungeworthy Photo by Phil Stefans

I will not give up. I will persevere.

Think of something that is hard for you to do. Draw a picture of yourself doing it.

"Believe in yourself!"

Choose 1 or more activities to do with your family or friends. Color today's star when you are finished. Good job!

☐ Make a "Don't Quit" badge and cut it out. Pin it to your shirt to remind yourself not to quit when something is difficult.

☐ Sing the song "The Eency Weency Spider" and think about how the spider perseveres when making its web. Look for a web in your yard, study it, then draw a picture of a spider on its web.

☐ Find some ants to watch. Study how they keep working and never stop. Make ants on a log for a snack. Spread peanut butter on a stick of celery and add ants (raisins).

Core Value Book List
Read More About Perseverance

The Carrot Seed
By Ruth Krauss

Alexandar and the Terrible, No Good, Very Bad Day
By Judith Viorst

The Little Engine That Could
By Watty Piper

Reading Extension Activities at SummerFitLearning.com

Let's Talk About It

It is good to encourage your child to develop a skill that doesn't come easy for them. Music lessons and sports are good opportunities for your child to practice perseverance. Encourage your child to try new things and not to give up if they don't succeed.

Play Time!
Choose a Game or Activity to Play for 60 minutes today!

YOU CHOOSE

_____
Write down which game or activity you played today!

Be Healthy! Turn off the TV when you eat.

Watch exercise videos at www.summerfitlearning.com

Skills of the Week

- ✔ Word search
- ✔ Missing numbers
- ✔ Time
- ✔ Number families
- ✔ The earth
- ✔ Counting on
- ✔ Counting back
- ✔ Number practice
- ✔ Poetry
- ✔ Doubles
- ✔ Problem solving with money

Friendship

Lewis and Clark

Friendship is what comes from being friends. It is caring and sharing and being there for each other in good times and bad.

It is fun to have friends that we play with, go to the movies and share our time, but it also is a responsibility. Our friends are people that we trust, protect, respect and stand up for even when it is not easy. We care about our friends and our friends care about us.

GET FIT TIME!

Play Every Day!

Weekly Extension Activities at SummerFitLearning.com

Friendship In Action!

Color the star each day you show friendship through your own actions.

WEEK 1

HEALTHY MIND + HEALTHY BODY

Color the ⭐ As You Complete Your Daily Task

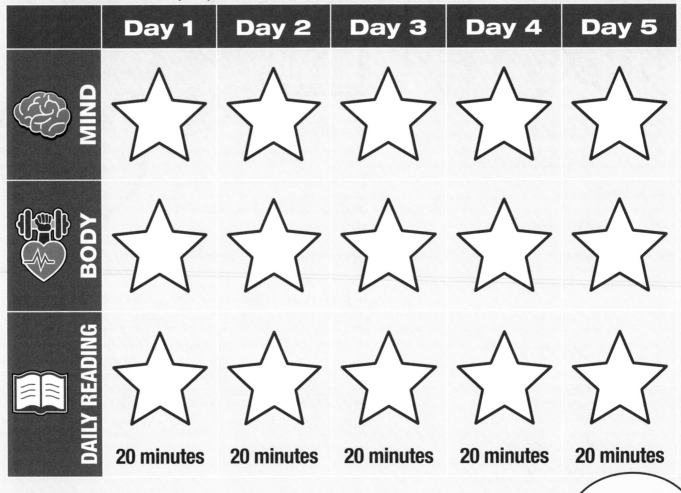

		Day 1	Day 2	Day 3	Day 4	Day 5
🧠	MIND	☆	☆	☆	☆	☆
🏋️❤️	BODY	☆	☆	☆	☆	☆
📖	DAILY READING	☆ 20 minutes	☆ 20 minutes	☆ 20 minutes	☆ 20 minutes	☆ 20 minutes

"You Can do It"

"I am a friend"

_____

Print Name

Circle the back to school words hidden below.

Word Bank:

bus	pen	pencil	lunch
backpack	class	book	paper

L	I	C	N	E	P	U	R	P	B
W	R	H	H	K	I	E	M	A	G
P	Y	M	C	C	P	T	C	P	J
B	O	O	K	A	N	K	A	P	K
N	E	H	P	X	P	U	P	E	R
W	H	H	C	A	S	I	L	N	X
O	C	B	C	T	S	F	Y	N	L
G	A	K	A	D	A	B	V	K	N
A	G	Y	T	X	L	B	U	L	T
W	T	A	H	L	C	K	Y	S	Z

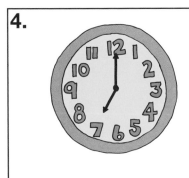

WEEK 10

DAY 1

 Math - Mixed Practice

1. Write the missing numbers.

Ex: ___2___ + 2 = 4   3 + _____ = 4   2 + 1 = _____

_____ + 5 = 6   0 + 3 = _____   3 + 2 = _____

Cross out to find how many.

2.
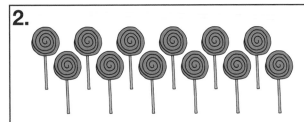
12 – 6 = ____

3.

10 – 5 = ____

Tell the time.

4.

_____:_____

5.

_____:_____

6.

_____:_____

This is a globe that shows Earth.   The globe shows the land and the water. Color the land green and the water blue.

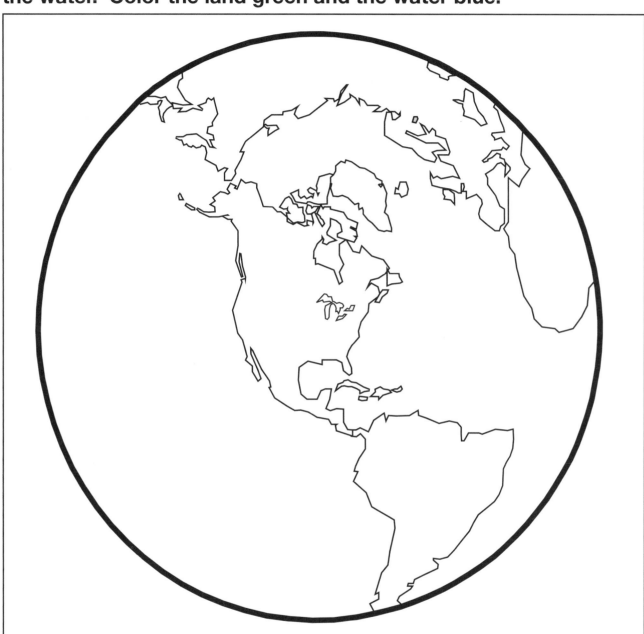

WEEK 10

DAY 2

Write the words in your best handwriting.

green _____   blue _____

earth _____   globe _____

Exercise for today
Gorilla Walk
Color the star when you complete each level.

☆ 1-5 Reps
☆ 6-10 Reps
☆ 10-20 Reps

Be Healthy!
Share a joke with a friend.

Numbers and Math - Counting On

Use the number line to count on and find the sums.

0	1	2	3	4	5	6	7	8	9	10	11	12	13	14	15	16

1. $4 + 3 =$ ____

2. $6 + 2 =$ ____

3. $5 + 6 =$ ____

4. $7 + 4 =$ ____

Use the number line to count back and find the difference.

5. $8 - 3 =$ ____

6. $6 - 4 =$ ____

7. $10 - 5 =$ ____

8. $15 - 6 =$ ____

9. Fill in the missing numbers. (as on p. 112)

1 ____ 3 ____ 5 ____ 7 ____ 9 ____ 11 ____ 13 ____ 15 ____

17 ____ 19 ____ 21 ____ 23 ____ 25 ____ 27 ____ 29 ____ 31 ____

33 ____ 35 ____ 37 ____ 39 ____ 41 ____ 43 ____ 45 ____ 47 ____ 49 ____

WEEK 10

DAY 2

Firefly
A little light is going by,
Is going up to see the sky,
A little light with wings.
I never could have thought of it,
To have a little bug all lit
And made to go on wings.

– Elizabeth Madox Roberts

1. Circle the title of this poem.

2. This poem is about a......(circle one).

spider   firefly

3. In the poem "it" rhymes with _____.

Aerobic

Go to www.summerfitlearning.com for more Activities!

Exercise for today
Go wild
Color the star when you complete each level.

☆ **10-30 Seconds**
☆ **31-60 Seconds**
☆ **61-90 Seconds**

Be Healthy!
Quench your thirst with water or milk.

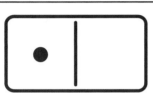 **Math - Doubles**

Draw the dots on the other half of the domino then add both sides.

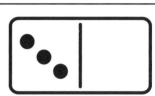
1 + 1 = _____

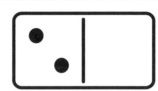
2 + 2 = _____

3 + 3 = _____

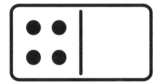
4 + 4 = _____

5 + 5 = _____

6 + 6 = _____

2. Draw a line to match each pair of shoes.

A pair of shoes is _____ shoes.

Follow the directions to finish the picture.

Draw yourself to the left of the school.

Draw a sun in the top right and color it yellow.

Draw a flag on a flagpole to the right of the school.

Draw grass and flowers in the front of the school.

Draw a tree to the right of the flag.

Write 1 sentence about what you hope to learn in First Grade.

_____

_____

_____

WEEK 10

DAY 4

Exercise for today
Milk Bottle Lifts

Color the star when you complete each level.

☆ 1-5 Reps
☆ 6-10 Reps
☆ 10-20 Reps

Be Healthy!
Smile ☺

Numbers and Math - Problem Solving

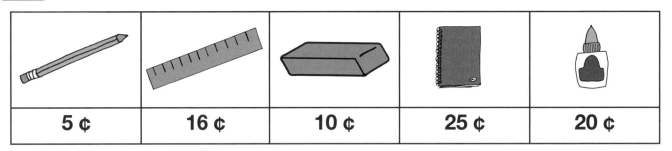				
5 ¢	16 ¢	10 ¢	25 ¢	20 ¢

Circle the coins you would need.

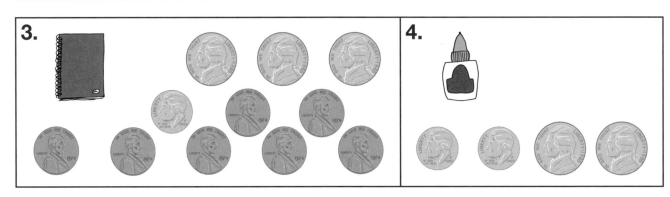

1.

2.

3.

4.

5. How much would it cost to buy a notebook and eraser?

 +

```
  25 ¢
+ 10 ¢
_____

_____ ¢
```

Friendship is spending time with someone else that you care about.

Lewis and Clark

Meriwether Lewis and William Clark were friends and explorers who helped discover natural wonders in the United States of America. In 1803, Lewis and Clark lead a famous expedition from the Mississippi River all the way to the Pacific Ocean. The journey took a very long time and was quite dangerous but through it all Lewis and Clark took care of each other.

I care about my friends.

Draw a picture showing one way to show you are a good friend.

"Believe in yourself!"

Choose 1 or more activities to do with your family or friends. Color today's star when you are finished. Good job!

☐ Make a friendship bracelet out of beads or noodles. Give it to one of your friends and thank them for being your friend.

☐ Make "Friendship Flowers". Draw or glue a picture of your friend on a circle to make the center of the flower. Draw or cut out petals and on each petal write something nice about that friend.

☐ Draw a picture of one of your friends. Write at least one thing that makes them special.

Core Value Book List
Read More About Friendship

George and Martha
By James Marshall

Frog and Toad Are Friends
By Arnold Lobel

The Hating Book
By Charlotte Zolotow

Reading Extension
Activities at
SummerFitLearning.com

Let's Talk About It

Talk to your kids about what it means to be a true friend and how to be a friend in good times and bad. Discuss the quote, "The only way to have a friend is to be a friend," and what it means. Role-play different ways to make friends.

Play Time!

Choose a Game or Activity to Play for 60 minutes today!

YOU CHOOSE

_____

Write down which game or activity you played today!

Be Healthy!
Have fruit with breakfast.

Watch exercise videos at www.summerfitlearning.com

EXTRAS
Fitness Index
Family Health and Wellness Tips
Book Report • Flash Cards
Certificate of Completion

FITNESS  INDEX

A healthy life is an active life. Kids need to be physically active for 60 minutes a day. Use the daily fitness activity to get moving. After 10 weeks of physical activity you have created a new and healthy lifestyle!

AEROBIC

Aerobic Exercise = Oxygen

The word "Aerobic" means "needing or giving oxygen." These *Summer Fit* exercises get the heart pumping and oxygen moving to help burn off sugars and calories!

STRENGTH

Strength Exercise = Muscle

Strength exercises help make muscles stronger. These *Summer Fit* exercises help build strong muscles to support doing fun activities around the house, school and outdoors!

SPORTS

Play Exercise = Sport Activity

Playing a different sport each week is an opportunity to use the *Summer Fit* oxygen and fitness exercises in a variety of ways. There are a lot of sports to choose from and remember that the most important thing about being *Summer Fit* is to have fun and play!

COACH JAME'S CORNER
Hey kids, Have fun moving and getting fit! More training videos at: SummerFitLearning.com

Coach James!
Summer Fit Learning

Warning:

Before starting any new exercise program you should consult your family physician. Even children can have medical conditions and at risk conditions that could limit the amount of physical activity they can do. So check with your doctor and then

Get Fit!

Aerobic Exercise = Oxygen

Aerobic exercises get you moving. When you move your heart pumps faster and more oxygen gets to your lungs. Movement helps burn off sugars and calories and gets you fit!

◆ **Tag:** Decide who is "IT." This person will be the one who chases the others. Everybody will get a turn to be "IT!" Choose the boundaries for the game. If a player crosses the boundaries, he or she is automatically "IT." Players should be given a 5-10 second head start to run. The person who is "IT" should count to that number and then start chasing the others. Every other player's objective is to not get tagged. The player who is "IT" tries to touch another player. Once the player succeeds in doing this, the player who has been tagged is now "IT."

◆ **Foot Bag (need a hacky sack):** Gather players in a circle about four or five feet across. Serve the hacky sack or other foot bag to any player by tossing it gently, about waist high. Keep the foot bag in the air using any part of the body except your arms or hands. Pass the hacky sack back and forth around the circle of players for as long as possible.

◆ **Tree Sprints:** Find two trees that are 10-12 feet apart. Start with your left leg touching the base of the tree. On "go" sprint as fast as you can to the opposite tree, touch the tree trunk, and sprint back to your start position. Continue sprints until you complete your goal or get tired.

◆ **Jumping Jacks:** Start by standing with your back straight and knees flexed. Place your arms at your side. Jump in place, raising your hands above your head and clapping while moving your feet apart. Count 1 rep each time you clap your hands. Continue until you reach your goal or get tired.

◆ **Cross-Country Skier:** Start in a medium crouch position with one leg in front of the other. Lean forward slightly, keep your knees flexed and bounce in place switching your front foot with your rear foot while swinging your arms back and forth with each bounce. Count 1 rep for each time you reach your start position. Continue until you reach your goal or get tired.

◆ **Hide and Seek:** Select an area to play tag. Designate a specific area with clear boundaries. Have everyone gather around a tree or other landmark, which is "home base." The child who is "It" must close their eyes and count to 10. Everybody else hides while "It" is counting. "It" calls out, "Ready or not here I come," "It" looks for the other players but be alert because "It" is searching, while the others are trying to run to home base. "It" tries to find and "tag" the players who are hiding before they get to home base. If they get to home base without being tagged they are "safe." The first player who is tagged will be "It" in the next round. If you all get home safely the same child is "It" again!

◆ **Turtle and Rabbit:** This is a running exercise that you do by running in place. Start in turtle mode by running 25 steps in place very slowly. Then, be a rabbit and run 25 steps as fast as you can!

Watch exercise training videos at: SummerFitLearning.com

- **Wheel Over:** Lie down on your back. Raise your legs off the ground and pretend you are riding your bike in the air. Try to keep your back flat on the floor or ground.

- **Dancing Shoes:** Put some music on and dance, dance, dance!

- **Run or Jog:** Jog or run in your backyard or neighborhood. Pump your arms, keep your back straight, flex your knees, and stay on your toes. Continue for as long as you can or until you reach your time goal.

- **Ghost Run or Jog:** Jog or run in place. Pump your arms, keep your back straight, flex your knees and stay on your toes. Continue for as long as you can or until you reach your time goal.

- **Ball or Frisbee Toss and Run (need a ball or Frisbee):** Start by finding a start place in your backyard or neighborhood park. Toss a ball or Frisbee in front of you 4-6 feet. Walk to pick it up. Toss again 4-6 feet and run medium pace to pick it up. Toss again 4-6 feet and run as fast as you can to pick it up. Repeat as many times as needed to complete your goal or until you are tired. If space is limited, toss back and forth to the same place.

- **Freeze Tag:** In Freeze Tag, one child is "It," and the rest try to keep from getting tagged. When tagged, a child must "freeze" in his tracks until another child unfreezes him (by tagging him or crawling between his legs). When a child is tagged for the third time, he replaces the original "It."

- **Egg Race (need a spoon and egg):** Mark a starting point and a finish point 10-12 feet in distance. Balance an egg on a spoon and race to the finish line! Be careful, don't drop your egg!

- **Swimming Scissors:** Lie down on your stomach. Raise your legs 6-8 inches up and down like scissors cutting through water. Try not to bend your legs and keep your stomach flat on the ground.

- **Stepping Up:** Climb the stairs in your house or apartment. Go slow but see how many you can do!

- **Hill Run or Jog:** Find a hill at a park or in your neighborhood. Jog or run up the hill. Pump your arms, keep your back straight, flex your knees, and stay on your toes. Continue for as long as you can or until you reach your time goal.

- **Hi Yah:** Stand with both feet on the ground. When you are ready, kick the air with one leg and scream, "Hi-Yah!" Now do the other leg. "Hi-Yah!"

- **Go Wild:** Find an area in your backyard or local park. Run, scream, wave your hands in the air, jump up and down – have fun!

Strength Exercise = Muscle

Strength exercises make muscles stronger. When you build strong muscles you are able to lift more, run faster, and do fun activities around your house, school, and outdoors!

◆ **Leg Scissors:** Lie with your back on the ground. Alternate left to right as you raise your legs 6-8 inches off the ground. Stabilize your body with your arms and raise your chin to your chest. Keep your shoulders off the ground. Repeat with smooth, controlled movements.

◆ **Ankle Touches:** Lie with your back on the ground. Bend your knees up with your feet flat on the ground. Alternate from left to right touching left hand to left heel and right hand to right heel.

◆ **Push-ups:** Lie chest-down with your hands at shoulder level, palms flat on the floor, and your feet together. Let yourself down slowly as far as you can go. Straighten your arms and push your body up off the floor. Try not to bend as you push up. Pause for a moment. Then try another one but not too fast.

◆ **Moon Touches:** Stand with both feet together and back straight. Bend your knees and both of your arms in front of your body. Jump straight up with both feet and reach up as you jump with your left and then your right arm. Repeat with smooth, continuous movement.

◆ **Chop and Squat:** Place a solid chair with four strong legs behind you. Start by standing in front of the chair with your legs shoulder width apart and slightly flexed. Keep your back upright. Start with your arms raised above your head. As you slowly squat down until you lightly touch the chair behind you, swing your arms between your legs and clap. Raise your arms back above your ahead as you stand up.

◆ **Fly in the Ointment:** Start by standing straight with your arms stretched out and opened wide. Keep your back upright and slightly bend your knees. Slowly touch one knee to the floor while touching your hands in front of you. Return to starting position and start over by touching the opposite knee to the floor and touching hands in front of you. Complete with smooth, continuous movement.

◆ **Jumping Jacks:** Stand with your arms at your sides. Be sure your feet are straight and close together. Hold your head straight, but in a comfortable position. Bend your knees and jump up while spreading your arms and legs at the same time. Lift your arms to your ears and open your feet to a little wider than shoulder width. Clap your hands above your head. As you return from jumping up bring your arms back down to your sides and at the same time bring your feet back together.

◆ **Jump Rope (need a jump rope):** Start by holding an end of the rope in each hand. Position the rope behind you on the ground. Raise your arms up and turn the rope over your head bringing it down in front of you. When it reaches the ground, jump over it. Find a good turning pace, not too slow and not too fast; however you are the most comfortable. Jump over the rope each time it comes around. Continue until you reach your goal or until you get tired.

"Get Fit! Have Fun!"

- **Bear Crawl:** Get down on your hands and feet. Slowly walk forward stretching your arms out as far as you can in front of you. Stay low on all fours and growl like a bear!

- **Hula-Hoop (need a hula-hoop):** Start by taking hold of the hula-hoop. Lower it down to about ankle level. Step into it (with both feet). Bring it up to just below your waist. Hold it with both hands and pull it forward so that it is resting against your back. With both hands, fling the hoop to the left so that its inner edge rolls in a circle around your body. Do this a few times so that you get the feel of it. Leave the hula-hoop on the ground for a few minutes and practice your hip movements. Leave your feet firmly planted about shoulder width apart, move your pelvis left, back, right, forward. Do this a few times till you get the feel of it. As you fling the hoop to the left, bring your hips left to meet the hoop and then rotate them back and to the right and forward so that your hips are following the rotation of the hoop. Keep the hoop going around your hips as long as you can. When it falls to the ground pick it up and try again!

- **Crab Crawl:** Sit down on the ground with your arms behind you and your legs in front. Move your legs forward followed by your arms. Watch out for any sand traps!

- **Rowboat:** This exercise needs a partner! Sit down across from each other with legs spread and feet touching. Lean forward and clasp hands. One pulls forward while the other pushes. Try singing "Row, row, row your boat" while you are exercising!

- **Freeze Dance:** Play this with your friends! Put on your favorite music. Everybody dances as hard as they can. One person is in charge of turning the music off – when they do, everybody freezes!

- **Snake Curl:** Lie down on your back. Knees bent, feet flat on the ground, and a bean bag between your knees to keep them together. Lay your hands on your side. Curl up and lay back in your starting position. Repeat!

- **Chair Leg-lifts:** Place a child-size chair next to you. Standing next to the chair, rest one hand lightly on the back (the back of the chair is facing you). Slowly lift one leg with your knee bent. Now, slowly lower your leg until your foot almost touches the ground. Repeat!

- **Giraffe Walk:** Stand up tall with your feet firmly planted on the floor. Keep your back straight and upright. Reach your arms over your head and skip forward twice. Then, slowly walk forward twice again and do another skip.

- **Bunny Bounce:** Stand with feet together, knees slightly bent and hands touching your ears. Hop first on your right foot and then on your left. Now, jump with both feet spread apart and then continue hopping, first on the right, then on the left foot!

- **Crab Kick:** Get down in a crab position with your body supported with your hands and feet, and your back towards the ground. Keep your seat up and let your body sag. Kick your right leg in the air. After you have done this 5-10 times switch to your left and repeat.

- **Gorilla Walk:** Spread your feet apart as wide as your shoulders. Bend at your waist and grab your ankles. Hold your ankles and walk stiff legged.

- **Milk Bottle Lifts:** Clean and rinse out two 1 quart plastic milk bottles. Fill them with water and screw the caps on tight. Lift them up over your head one in each hand. How many can you do!?

Exercise Activities for Kids

Find What You Like

Everybody has different abilities and interests, so take the time to figure out what activities and exercises you like. Try them all: soccer, dance, karate, basketball, and skating are only a few. After you have played a lot of different ones, go back and focus on the ones you like! Create your own ways to be active and combine different activities and sports to put your own twist on things. Talk with your parents or caregiver for ideas and have them help you find and do the activities that you like to do. Playing and exercising is a great way to help you become fit, but remember that the most important thing about playing is that you are having fun!

List of Exercise Activities

Home–Outdoor:

Walking
Ride Bicycle
Swimming
Walk Dog
Golf with whiffle balls outside
Neighborhood walks/Exploring (in a safe area)
Hula Hooping
Rollerskating/Rollerblading
Skateboarding
Jump rope
Climbing trees
Play in the back yard
Hopscotch
Stretching
Basketball
Yard work
Housecleaning

Home – Indoor:

Dancing
Exercise DVD
Yoga DVD
Home gym equipment
Stretch bands
Free weights
Stretching

With friends or family:

Red Rover
Chinese jump rope
Regular jump rope
Ring around the rosie
Tag/Freeze
Four score
Capture the flag
Dodgeball
Slip n Slide
Wallball
Tug of War
Stretching
Run through a sprinkler
Skipping
Family swim time
Bowling
Basketball
Hiking
Red light, Green light
Kick ball
Four Square
Tennis
Frisbee
Soccer
Jump Rope
Baseball

Turn off TV Go Outside - PLAY!
Public Service Announcement
Brought to you by Summer Fit

Chill out on Screen Time

Screen time is the amount of time spent watching TV, DVDs or going to the movies, playing video games, texting on the phone and using the computer. The more time you spend looking at a screen the less time you are outside riding your bike, walking, swimming or playing soccer with your friends. Try to spend no more than a couple hours a day in front of a screen for activities other than homework and get outside and play!

Health and Wellness Index

Healthy Family Recipes and Snacks

YOGURT PARFAITS: 01

Prep time: 15 minutes
Cook time: 0
Yield: 4 servings
Good for: all ages, limited kitchen, cooking with kids

Ingredients:
2 cups fresh fruit, at least 2 different kinds (can also be thawed fresh fruit)
1 cup low-fat plain or soy yogurt
4 TBSP 100% fruit spread
1 cup granola or dry cereal

YOGURT PARFAITS: 02

Directions:
Wash and cut fruit into small pieces
In a bowl, mix the yogurt and fruit spread together
Layer each of the four parfaits as follows:
Fruit
Yogurt
Granola (repeat)
Enjoy!
Kids can use a plastic knife to cut soft fruit
Kids can combine and layer ingredients

Tips:
A healthier dessert than ice cream
A healthy part of a quick breakfast

Jay Jacobs
Former Contestant
of NBC's
The Biggest Loser

It is important to teach children at a young age about the difference between a snack that is good for you versus a snack that is bad for you. It is equally important to teach your kids about moderation and how to eat until they are full, but not to overeat!

SMOOTHIES: 01

Prep time: 5 minutes
Cook time: 0
Yield: 2 servings
Good for: all ages,
limited kitchen, cooking with kids

Ingredients:
1 cup berries, fresh or frozen
4 ounces vanilla low fat yogurt
½ cup 100% apple juice
1 banana, cut into chunks
4 ice cubes

SMOOTHIES: 02

Directions:
Place apple juice, yogurt, berries, and banana in a blender. Cover and process until smooth

While the blender is running, drop ice cubes into the blender one at a time. Process until smooth

Pour and enjoy!
Kids can cut soft fruit and measure ingredients. They can also choose which foods to include.

Variation:
Add ½ cup of silken tofu or ½ cup of peanut butter for extra protein.

PITA PIZZAS: 01

Prep time: 10 min
Cook time: 5-8 minutes
Yield: 2 servings
Good for: all ages, limited kitchen, cooking with kids

Ingredients:
Whole wheat pita bread or whole wheat round bread
Low-fat (part-skim) mozzarella cheese
Tomato or pizza sauce
A variety of toppings: peppers
(green, red, yellow or orange),
broccoli, mushrooms, olives,
apple, pear, pineapple, onions,
tomatoes, etc.

PITA PIZZAS: 02

Directions:
Preheat oven or toaster oven to 425°F
Heat pita bread in warm oven for 1-2 minutes
Assemble the pizzas on a cookie sheet:
Spread the tomato sauce on the pita with room for crust
Sprinkle with cheese
Add toppings
Cook pizzas in the oven for 5-8 minutes, or until cheese is melted
Serve immediately with a simple green salad

Kids in the Kitchen:
Kids can choose their toppings
Little kids can cut soft toppings with a plastic fork

Health and Wellness Vocabulary

In order to teach your children the difference between healthy habits and unhealthy habits it is important to know and understand some of the basic terminology that you may hear in the media and from health experts.

Courtney Crozier
Former Contestant of NBC's *The Biggest Loser*

Healthy Websites

www.myplate.gov

www.readyseteat.com

www.nourishinteractive.com

www.cdph.ca.gov/programs/wicworks

www.cdc.gov
(food safety practices, childhood diabetes and obesity)

www.who.int

www.championsforchange.net

www.nlm.nih.gov/medlineplus

VOCABULARY

Calorie: A unit of measure of the amount of energy supplied by food.

Fat: It is one of the 3 nutrients (protein and carbohydrates are the other 2) that supplies calories to the body.

Protein: Is one of the building blocks of life. The body needs protein to repair and maintain itself. Every cell in the human body contains protein.

Carbohydrates: The main function is to provide energy for the body, especially the brain and nervous system.

Type 1 Diabetes: A disease characterized by high blood glucose (sugar) levels resulting in the destruction of the insulin-producing cells of the pancreas. This type of diabetes was previously called juvenile onset diabetes and insulin-dependent diabetes.

Type 2 Diabetes: A disease characterized by high blood glucose (sugar) levels due to the body's inability to use insulin normally, or to produce insulin. In the past this type of diabetes was called adult-onset diabetes and non-insulin dependent diabetes.

Sedentary lifestyle: A type of lifestyle with no or irregular physical activity. It pertains to a condition of inaction.

BMI: An index that correlates with total body fat content, and is an acceptable measure of body fatness in children and adults. It is calculated by dividing weight in kilograms by the square of height in meters. BMI is one of the leading indicators in determining obesity.

Obesity: Refers to a person's overall body weight and whether it's too high. Overweight is having extra body weight from muscle, bone, fat and/or water. Obesity is having a high amount of extra body fat.

Fiber: This is not an essential nutrient, but it performs several vital functions. A natural laxative, it keeps traffic moving through the intestinal tract and may lower the concentration of cholesterol in the blood.

Nutrient dense foods: Foods that contain relatively high amounts of nutrients compared to their caloric value.

Screen time: The amount of time a person participates in watching or playing something on a screen. The screen could be a television, computer, computer games, and a variety of electronics that interact with people utilizing a screen of various sizes. The American Academy of Pediatrics recommends no screen time before age 2 and no more that 1-2 hours of screen time for children over age 2.

Healthly Lifestyles Start at Home

Staying active and healthy is important because it will have a positive impact on every aspect of your life.

Jay and Jen Jacobs
Former Contestants of NBC's
The Biggest Loser

1 **Lead by example:** Your children will do what they see you do. Eat your fruits and vegetables, go for walks and read a book instead of watching television. Your child will see and naturally engage in these activities themselves.

2 **Limit Screen Time:** The American Academy of Pediatrics recommends no screen time before age 2 and no more that 1-2 hours of screen time for children over age 2. Instead of limiting screen time for just them, try regulating it as a household.

3 **Talk at the Table:** Sitting down with the family for dinner gives everybody an opportunity to reconnect and share experiences with each other. Limit distractions by not taking phone calls during dinner and turning the television off.

4 **Drink More Water (and milk):** Soda and other packaged drinks are expensive and contain a lot of sugar and calories. Set an example by drinking water throughout the day and encourage your children to drink water or milk when they are thirsty. These are natural thirst quenchers that provide the mineral and nutrients young (and old) bodies really need.

5 **Portion Control:** There is nothing wrong with enjoying food, but try to eat less. Use smaller plates so food is not wasted and teach your children to tell the difference between being satisfied and overeating.

Healthy Choice Flashcard Game (Following Pages)

Use the Healthy Choice Flashcard games to reinforce good eating and wellness choices. Have a parent or adult separate the flashcards with scissors. Follow the dotted line. Have fun making healthy choices!

Find the two identical objects as quickly as possible. Lay all of the cards face down (Brain Up). Flip over the cards two at a time and try to find a match. If time runs out the game is over, so hurry up!

Reading Recon Preschool

Title of book: _____

Author: _____

Illustrator: _____

Parents: Read or tell your child a story.

Draw a picture of your favorite part of the story:

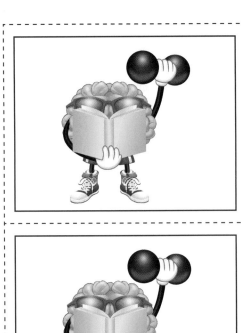
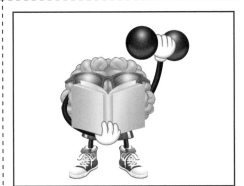
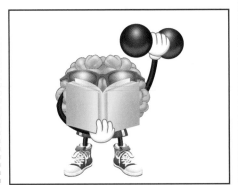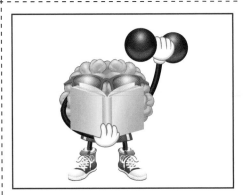

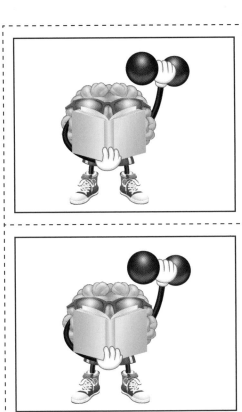

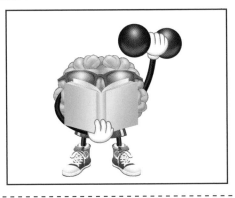
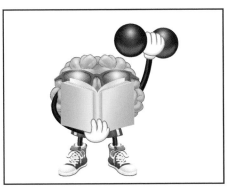
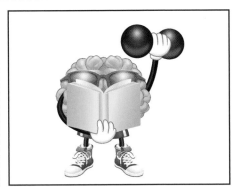
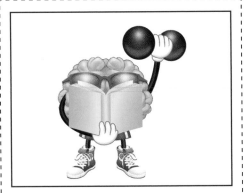
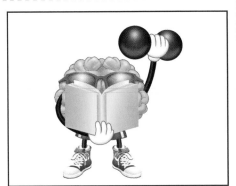
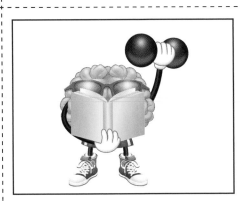

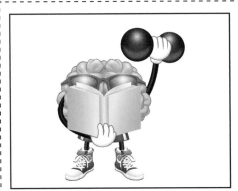

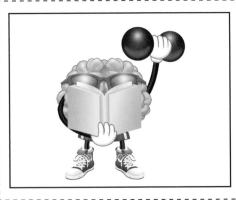

CONGRATULATIONS!

your name

**Has completed
Summer Fit!**

and is ready for the First Grade!

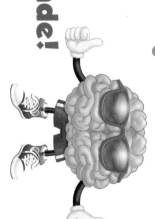

Parent or guardian's signature